Modern American Drama:

Essays in Criticism

Edited by
WILLIAM E. TAYLOR

EVERETT/EDWARDS, INC.
DeLAND, FLORIDA 32720

1st Edition April, 1968

Book Design by Bill Brinkworth

———

Manufactured in the United States of America
by Convention Press, Inc., Jacksonville, Florida

In Appreciation,
Dedicated to
CRAWFORD SOLOMON
Printer, Publisher,
Patron of the Arts

Modern American

Drama:

Essays in Criticism

Contents

Introduction

In 1906, William Vaughn Moody's play, *The Great Divide,*
was hailed as the most significant contribution that had ever been
made to the American drama, and it held this position until the
advent of Eugene O'Neill. If we look back on *The Great Divide*
from the 60's, however, we see it with entirely different eyes.
We may be inclined to wonder how anybody could have taken it
seriously. We may observe that it has most of the ingredients of
present-day scripts for Western epics of the silver screen, or, worse,
that it is now being rewritten fifty to a hundred times a week for the
mass audiences of television. It has all the cliches: a good-man-gone-
bad who is salvaged and becomes a millionaire because of his love
for a beautiful and virtuous girl, a heroine who loves the beauty of
life but her honor more, a conflict between Puritanical obsession
with sin and romantic faith in the instinctive goodness of the human heart, and, above all, a happy ending announcing the triumph
of goodness over evil in the great American dream, the second chance
—"out West" —beyond the great divide.

The plot of this play concerns Ruth Jordan, who is left alone
one night in the cabin of her brother Philip, a young New Englander
who has gone west to make his fortune. Three drunken saddle
tramps break into the cabin with the intention of raping her. She
pleads for mercy and offers herself to whichever will save her
from the others. Stephen Ghent, the hero, accepts her offer. He
buys off one of his cohorts with a necklace of gold nuggets and
shoots it out with the other. He claims his reward, telling Ruth to
pack her things and ride off with him. She begs him to reconsider,

1

in words that sound strange to anyone who has read an American play by Eugene O'Neill, Tennessee Williams, or Edward Albee:

> You will be merciful. You will not hold me to *my cruel oath.* [Italics mine.]

She discovers, however, that Ghent intends to do just that. In the second act, which takes place an undetermined number of years later, Ghent has struck gold and has tried to win Ruth's love by buying her diamond necklaces and having an architect draw plans for a magnificent house. But Ruth is adamant. She has been bought—they were married, of course, immediately after her abduction—for a necklace of gold nuggets, and she spends all her spare time weaving baskets and rugs to sell at a nearby tourist trap in order to buy herself back. Though she is pregnant, she throws Ghent's gifts into the canyon and refuses to look at the plans for the house. Her brother Philip turns up at the hotel on his way back east after failing to make a go of it without Ruth's help, and discovers her among the Indians, selling her wares to the tourists. He accosts Ghent. If Ghent is so rich, he wants to know, "Why, then is my sister compelled to peddle her own handiwork in a public caravansery?" Ghent is aghast. But Ruth tells him the truth, returns to him the necklace of nuggets, which she bought back from Ghent's erstwhile competitor for her possession. Having freed herself, she leaves her husband and returns to New England with her bankrupt and ineffectual brother.

In Act II, we are in the Jordan New England home. Ruth is ill—if she only knew it, pining away for her husband. Her mother, however, has conspired with Ghent, who is secretly nearby, has paid off the mortgage, and has even bought up Philip's western claim, worked it, made it a success, and given it to the Jordans—all without Ruth's knowledge. The mother wishes to bring the two lovers together again and brings Stephen into the house to confront Ruth. In a passion of despair, Ruth finally reveals to her mother and her brother the conditions of her marriage. The reactions are interesting. Philip is outraged, wants to fight it out with Ghent, "He'll answer to me!" he cries. But the two men are kept from fighting. The mother's reaction is dramatized as follows:

Mrs. Jordan: *cold and rigid* And you—married him—after that?
She starts away in horror-stricken judgement. You ought to have—died—first!

*Philip opens the door and enters, staring at Ghent with dis-
like and menace.*
Oh Philip, she has told me!—You can't imagine what hor-
rors!

Ghent and Ruth are, for some reason, left alone at this point.
He tries to persuade her that she should return West with him,
that their love is the important thing. She feels that their love has
never had a chance to become real because of the way it started.
Speaking of her mother's words, she says, "She spoke the truth.
I have always seen it." Ghent should have seen, she says, that "the
wages of sin is death" and that they had to be purified through suffering before their marriage could be successful and happy. He replies that a few days ago he had stepped into "one of your meeting
houses" and heard the preacher speak of "The Second Birth." That,
he claims, is what happened to him, years ago, when they were married. He became a new man, but she would not see it. "Suffering,"
he continues,

> may be the law for some, and I've tried hard to see it as
> our law, and I thought I had succeeded. But I haven't! Our
> law is joy, and selfishness; the curve of your shoulder and
> the light on your hair as you sit there says that as plain as
> preaching.

Ruth sees the light and says, "You have taken the good of our life
and grown strong. I have taken the evil and grown weak, weak unto
death. Teach me to live as you do!" She puts the chain about her
neck, and the two live happily ever after—beyond the Great Divide.

The theme of *The Great Divide* is crucial to the American
literary tradition—the basic schizophrenia in our culture caused by
the conflict between Romantic optimism and Puritanical pessimism,
that *bête noire* of so much current writing. But there is a difference
between the way, say, Edward Albee or Tennessee Williams deals
with the schism and the way Moody was able to deal with it. First,
Moody makes it sound rather easy. Of course, it causes his characters a good deal of trouble. However, we do not have the detailed
probing that Williams and Albee submit it to; nor will Williams or
Albee admit that the individual caught in the split can free himself from it, even with the help of such an apt symbol as the geo-
graphical great divide. As with Auden, the mountains of the mind,
to current writers who are prepared to deal with Freud as well as
Darwin, are not easily scaled.

And the language of Moody's play is dated. No contemporary playwright could have a character say in all seriousness, "You cannot hold me to my cruel oath." Think, for example, of the rape scene in *Streetcar Named Desire*. Stanley Kowalski says he and Blanche have had this date for a long time, and though we feel the horror of the violence and the pathos of its result we are inclined not to feel the moral outrage. It is too bad, but how right or how wrong is either Stanley or Blanche? Most modern readers —and the critics, too, for that matter—can approach such questions only tentatively, if at all.

What might a contemporary dramatist do with that first cabin scene in Moody's play? At least two things. He would in the first place seize upon it as a rare opportunity for some fine talk. Bernard Shaw said the old formula for a play was (1) exposition, (2) situation, and (3) unravelling. We now have, he said, (1) exposition, (2) situation, and (3) *discussion*.

Suppose, too, the modern playwright wishes to have a heroine full of puritanical repressions, what would he do? Ruth Jordan's love of life is expressed through her love for the beauty of the desert. A Tennessee Williams will recognize the female instinct to love life, too, but with him it will be thwarted by some kind of frustrated sex drive—as with Alma in *Summer and Smoke*, or Honey in Albee's *Who's Afraid of Virginia Woolf?*

Two influences, then, stand between the modern reader and the plays of William Vaughn Moody. First, of course, is the influence of European dramatists. One of the major contributions of the Washington Square Players and the Theatre Guild was to produce Ibsen, Chekov, Shaw, Strindberg, Kaiser, and others, giving American dramatists examples of the pathfinding in subject matter, in tone, in language, in structure, in experimental technique that American writers between 1890 and 1917 never dreamed of. They learned the dramatic significance of what John Gassner calls "environment" from, among others, Ibsen, who, it is said, would build miniature sets and move his characters about in them as he wrote his plays, so that he was creating a little world in which they could exist. Environment, of course, means more than the physical setting (the details about props, exits and entrances, lighting, sounds); it means the psychological, the social, and the economic setting that Ibsen and other Europeans saw as so vital a part of the character and plot.

The American playwrights also learned something about plot or structure from Chekov. At the end of Ibsen's *Hedda Gabler,* for example, the heroine commits suicide because she is trapped. Chekhov, as Eric Bentley has demonstrated by a comparison of the early and late versions of *Uncle Vanya,* had discovered that people for the most part do not act that way. When they are trapped and know it, they just live it out, day by inexorable day, through the tedium and boredom and futility of it all. Chekhov and Strindberg were expressing this aspect of life long before Beckett's *Waiting for Godot.*

This basic insight, of course, had implications for concepts of dramatic structure and helped to stimulate the search for new form, what Bernard Dukore calls in his essay "the new realism." The result is that a modern American play may not only *he* either realistic, naturalistic, expressionistic, but it may be all of these at different times or even at the same time. One result is that these terms lose their usefulness as critical counters, and the critic is almost forced to satisfy himself with the *explication de texte,* as in Max Halperen's analysis of Albee's plays. O'Neill is sometimes successful and sometimes not in blending naturalistic character with expressionistic settings and structure. Elmer Rice in *The Adding Machine* is writing an almost entirely expressionistic play with a naturalistic philosophy. In *Street Scene,* on the other hand, his naturalistic setting and technique take on the symbolic distortion of expressionism in Jo Mielziner's design for the 1929 Broadway production. Much the same happens in the design of the set for Maxwell Anderson's *Winterset.* There are two issues here: first, developments in the ability to probe character, conflict (internal and external), and theme affected the *expression* (the technique, the theory of what drama really is); and second, these same developments made dramatic modes (realism, naturalism, expressionism) obsolete as absolutes almost as soon as they were introduced to the American theatre. One must hasten to add, however, that a rather simple realism—not necessarily simpleminded—was able to survive all this in plays like Owen Davis's *Icebound* (1924) or Sidney Howard's *They Knew What They Wanted* (1924) or his *The Silver Cord* (1926) or Maxwell Anderson's *Saturday's Children* in the 30's, or the plays of Barry, Sherwood, and Behrman, who were able to use that realism in a highly distinctive—for American dramatists—manner; and George Kelly's *The Showoff* and *Craig's Wife* employed traditional realism in still another way, for writing domestic tragedies and comedies.

Besides their tendency to probe the more elemental aspects of life with a new complexity, the new American dramatists demonstrated revolutionary ideas about style. It began on a relatively obvious level, that of diction, though it is not unrelated to the more important issues I have just been discussing. In Anderson and Stalling's *What Price Glory?*, for instance, we have not only the unglamorized picture of war for the first time in American dramatic literature, but we have men talking about it in something approximating the language they would actually have used, initiating what has become the central issue of "polite" discussions of the so-called "moral decay" of modern literary art. The opposite, of course, is what has actually happened, and it began with an honesty in language to match the honesty of character and theme. In *What Price Glory?* for example, one character exclaims, "Why in God's name can't we all go home? Who gives a damn for this lousy, stinking little town but the poor French bastards who live here?" Innocent enough today, but at the time it was new.

Fortunately, profanity is not the essence of the stylistic revolution, even if it is often the hallmark. Mrs. Zero's monologue at the beginning of Rice's *The Adding Machine* is a fair illustration of what I mean. There is not only the exaggerated tendency to drop the "g" from "ing" and the "d" from "and"; there is the rhythm of the speech which rings true to the ear; there is the use of slang and clichés, the repetition of trite exclamations, the grammatical vulgarisms—all of which reflect and create a mean, shallow, vulgar mind. Let me quote just a sentence or two from Mrs. Zero: "Seven years since you got a raise! An' if you don't get one tomorrow, I'll bet a nickle you won't have the guts to go an' ask for one. I didn't pick much when I picked you, I'll tell the world. You ain't much to be proud of." Aside from the language here, there is prefiguring of that monstrosity, "the American Woman," who is to appear in many a later American play.

In *Street Scene* (1929), Rice's second major contribution to American dramatic literature, style is obviously an important tool in building the edifice of the play. There is, in the first place, an attempt to reproduce dialect: Swedish, Italian, and Jewish. The last of these has been most often commented on because, I suppose, Jewish speech is so frequently associated with street life in New York City —and *Street Scene* is primarily successful as a symphonic presentation of what that life is like. Another reason for the appeal of the Jewish accent in the play, however, is that it comes from one of the most sympathetic characters, old Abraham Kaplan, a home-spun philosopher who is against social injustices, bigotry, the exploitation of working classes by the capitalists, capital punishment, and what he calls "sax jealousy." Let me cite just one or two lines of dialogue. Late in the play, after Rose's father, Frank Maurant, has killed his wife and her lover, Kaplan remarks:

> How ken ve call ourselves civilized, ven ve see that sax jealousy hes de power to avaken in us de primitive pessions of de sevege?

And when Lippo observes that

> He'sa gonna gat de'lectrica chair, ha?

Kaplan answers,

> De blood-lust of our enlightened population must be satisfied! De Chreestian state will kerry out to de last letter de Mosaic law.

Rice also handles the clichés of the street with tact and effectiveness. The play takes place in the summer, and no place in the world is as hot in summer as New York City. As Rice slowly assembles his cast on the stoop of the tenement at the beginning of the first act (it is evening, just before supper, the ladies are hanging out the windows gossiping and the men are coming home from work), each one greets the others with the expression, "Well, is it hot enough for you?" This is unobtrusively and forcefully done. Other characters offer variation on the statement: "The trouble with a bath is, by the time you're all through, you're as hot as when you started" or "I was just saying to my wife, it's not the heat I mind as much as it is the humidity." Finally, Lippo enters, carrying five dripping ice cream cones and distributes them among the tenants, pulling his sticky shirt away from his sweating body as he does so.

Another stylistic device Elmer Rice employs in *Street Scene* is the use of off-stage sounds and on-stage intrusions, for lack of a better name. These reproduce speech-patterns from several social levels. For example, the first voice of the play is someone off-stage, calling "Char-lie!" This is repeated two or three times at different points in the play. Another off-stage sound is that of someone shouting, "Red rover, red rover, let Freddie come over." This is used twice. One workman is heard shouting to another in the basement of the adjacent building, which is being torn down.

The on-stage intrusions are equally interesting, sometimes being relevant to the action, as when two nursemaids at the beginning of Act III, after the murder, come by to stare at the house and locate the murder room by an exaggerated and lurid picture in the newspaper. Sometimes on-stage intrusions are completely unrelated to the action of the play, as when an old-clothes man comes on shouting, "I kesh ko! I kesh ko!" or a man comes on shouting *"Straw*-berries! Straw-*berries!"* or two girls cross the stage:

> First Girl: That I didn't know.
> Second Girl: Convex is this way; and concave if this way.
> First Girl: That I know.
> Second Girl: When you're near-sighted, they give you convex glasses, and when you're far-sighted, they give you concave.
> First Girl: That I didn't know.
> Second Girl: Of course, you know it. Didn't we have it in psychology?
> First Girl (as they disappear at the left) I don't remember.

In another place, a man and a woman enter wearing shorts and carrying tennis rackets.

> Woman: So I just looked at him for a moment, without saying anything. And then, I said, "My dear boy," I said. "What do you expect anyhow, in this day and age?" I said. "Why even Frankl has to do a black bathroom occasionally," I said.
> Man (as they disappear at the left): Exactly! And what did he say to that?

There are two effects accomplished by all this. In the first place, added to the gossip of the tenants, the variety of actions going on and counterpointed against the main action of the murder, all the off-stage sounds and the on-stage intrusions help give the play its density. *Street Scene* is, in the fullest sense of the term, a slice-of-life. From the evening of one day until the afternoon of the next we see and hear everything that takes place in front of a typical New York tenement. And this is a pleasing dramatic experience because Rice obviously knows what this is like and reproduces it with the fidelity of a quick eye and a sensitive ear.

In the second place, the verbal density of this play contributes to the theme. During the course of three acts, the audience sees a woman and her lover murdered by her husband, a woman and her two children dispossessed, their furniture put out on the street, another woman struggle all night to have a baby, two young people decide that they cannot marry because the young man must finish his study of law and if they were to marry their lives would end up just like all the other bickering, mean, and meaningless lives in the tenement. The audience has seen bigotry; it has seen a curious and bloodthirsty crowd form to see a murdered woman carried out on a stretcher; it has seen tenderness brutalized, yearning frustrated, all this to the dissonant counterpoint of the busy and disassociated energy of the turning life of a great city. At the end of the play, as a kind of coda from the strings, a group of children off-stage start singing "The Farmer in the Dell." This continues until the final curtain, which is brought down as "A sailor appears at the left with two girls, an arm about the waist of each. They stroll slowly across."

Elmer Rice's *The Adding Machine* and *Street Scene* illustrate another prominent concern of the 20's—social protest. In *They Knew What They Wanted,* for example, Joe, the migrant worker, is a card-carrying member of the I. W. W., the Wobblies. He is a striker and sees the solution to the class conflict in revolution. In *The Adding Machine* Mr. Zero is clearly a victim of a mechanized, industrial society that has robbed him of his humanity and made a cipher of him. In *Street Scene,* the liberal Abraham Kaplan sympathizes with the workers against the "keppitalists," advocates throwing off the yoke of exploitation, is called a red, and is told by his more conservative neighbors to go back to Russia where he came from. But in the plays of the 20's—and Elmer Rice is, after O'Neill, the writer most seriously and most deeply concerned with social problems—the cause of tragedy is not finally economic or social and the solution is not revolution. In *The Adding Machine* the fault is largely with Mr. Zero, himself. He does not have the sense to grasp happiness even when it is available to him. Rice, it seems, feels that tragedy—or the tragic life—results from the inadequacy of man's nature to cope with his environment. It is inherent, rather than external. This at least relates Rice thematically with the great tradition of European tragedy. In *Street Scene,* Rose Maurant and Sam Kaplan do not go off carrying white banners and shouting "Strike!" Instead, Rose rather quickly decides that she will try to find a place in the country where she can give her brother a better chance at happiness than she or her parents have had living in a city tenement. "The way I look at it," she tells Sam, "it's not what you do that matters so much; it's what you are."

In the theater of the 30s' there is a significant change. Two obvious causes are at work: first, of course, there is the Great Depression of the early years of the decade. The social criticism of Sidney Howard and Elmer Rice bursts into a blazing fury of social protest; and where Rice had been aware of social injustice, the writers of the 30's are infuriated by it and offer programs for its alleviation. The second factor that affects the drama of the 30's is the gathering clouds of war, the rise of Hitler's Nazi regime in Germany. Communism, a word today associated with all the terrorism of post-McCarthyism and fraught with the horrifying possibility of a Third World War which might very well bring with it total destruction, Communism in the 30's was a word which seemed a very real white hope in a country almost collapsed under the weight of economic depression. Communism was also thought of in the 30's as the political opposite of Nazi and Fascist totalitarianism. We need to keep this in mind when we read Robert Sherwood's *Idiot's Delight,* for example, or Lillian Hellman's *Watch on the Rhine,* or, more obviously, perhaps, any of the plays of Clifford Odets.

Odets is the playwright who most completely typifies the thunder of the 30's. He has its virtues and its weaknesses. He burst on the literary scene in 1935 with no fewer than four plays: *Waiting for Lefty, Till the Day I Die, Awake and Sing,* and *Paradise Lost.* Then he went to Hollywood, where, some critics think, he belonged. He returned to Broadway in 1937 with perhaps his best play, *Golden Boy;* in 1938, he offered *Rocket to the Moon.* Since then, four plays, *The Big Knife, Clash By Night, The Country Girl,* and *The Flowering Peach* have been received with mixed emotions by the critics— hope that each play would produce better things from a playwright with great talent but a disturbed and perhaps confused mind and spirit.

Odets got his start through his association with the Group Theatre, an organization led by Harold Clurman and modelled after the ideals of the Moscow Art Theatre. The most significant idea held by the Group Theatre Associates was that stage techniques, acting techniques, dramatic structure and experimentation were to be subordinated to the presentation of American life, American character, and contemporary social problems. There were to be no parts written for the Great Actor. There was to be no experimentation with technique for experiment's sake—only if a new form of expression was called for by the content of the play. This seems sound enough, the welding of content and form, but actually it was nothing of the sort. It was rather subordination of form to content, the sacrifice of art to idea.

The theater in the 20's and 30's had its moments and its artists. Realists like Owen Davis, Sidney Howard, and George Kelly kept alive a traditional mode for such new talents as that of Robert E. Sherwood and Lillian Hellman. The naturalist attitude and technique were absorbed into the American theater by such writers as Elmer Rice and Eugene O'Neill, but, most important, were not allowed to become stultifying limitations by either of these men. Expressionistic techniques were also attempted, used, and absorbed by O'Neill and Rice and became thereby tools of the American playwright. The result is that a contemporary American dramatist inherits a highly sophisticated technique, but can use it either completely or partially. If he prefers, he can employ time-honored approaches to the problems of the playwright. So far as language is concerned, the naturalistic influence was moulded into a "poetry of the streets" or "poetry of conversation" that has become, in the hands of a great talent like that of Tennessee Williams or Edward Albee, a delicate instrument for reproducing both the reality and the transcendence of man as animal.

Finally, playwrights of the 20's and 30's have left the contemporary theater a heritage of experiment that is powerful and useful because it was honest—an attempt to probe beneath the surface of the obvious to the outer limits of the human psyche. A student of the American theater today has a right to expect to see reproduced on the stage at least the complexity and the pathos of 20th century American life in a vehicle capable of containing it. That he may be more often disappointed than not, one is forced to admit. We may be able to say of American theater, as we can certainly say of American poetry, that it has come of age. That maturity may not be quite the thing of glory that the maturity of American poetry is. I personally think, however, it is better than most critics give it credit for being.

As for the essays in this book, a word or two about them and the structure they make when brought together may not be amiss. First of all, the authors of the essays had at the beginning of this project only one unifying idea presented to them by the editor: to show that the drama of this century is as vital and as important to our literature as the advances in poetry and fiction. I am not sure the case has been made, but certainly the idea was stimulating and instructive. It perhaps had something to do with the fact that these essays have a good deal to say about the playwrights' concern for the drama as an art form. The question of the value and validity of the dramatic mode is raised in the first essay on Eugene O'Neill by Jay L. Halio, is further questioned by my own essay comparing O'Neill and Pirandello, and turns up frequently in later discussions—in Shuman's essay on Odets, the essay on Maxwell Anderson, Sy Kahn's essay on Tennessee Williams, which is a poet's impassioned defense of poetic and dramatic freedom to express his deepest and most significant response to reality. The concern with the problem of dramatic technique is also in Bernard F. Dukore's discussion of Gelber in his essay on the Off-Broadway Theater, and it is implicit in many other essays in this book. It is, of course, the controlling concern of Alan Stambusky's essay on Arthur Miller.

Second, there is a remarkable constancy of thematic anguish reflected in these treatments of the modern drama in America. The theological concern persists after O'Neill in Tennessee Williams and Archibald MacLeish, though in more recent playwrights the problem is more implicit than explicit. The theme of individual integrity and the ability to communicate is basic to an understanding of Arthur Miller, but it is of significance to all the more recent dramatists, though especially, perhaps, to Carson McCullers, Edward Albee, James Baldwin, and Leroi Jones—in the latter two with perhaps a special twist of anguish and immediacy. The great themes of all time and all literature are present and being dealt with in terms of their peculiar modernity—the conflict between the feminine and male principles and the particular significance of each; the meaning of place or "home"; the problems of race; the threat of war. A specially interesting treatment of these, it seems to me, is offered by Weller Embler in his discussion of the comedy of manners that had a short glory in the 30's.

Finally, I would like to point out that all the essays in this book were written especially for it except Bernard Dukore's essay on the Off-Broadway Theater, which was originally written as a radio talk for the Voice of America; Sy Kahn's essay on Tennessee Williams, which was a talk delivered to an academic audience while the book was in preparation; and my own essay on O'Neill and Pirandello, which was a paper read before the Florida College English Association. All the other authors, of course, have special qualifications and interests, and perhaps stimuli, which made them particularly appropriate contributors in their special fields.   W. E. T.

Eugene O'Neill: the Long Quest

by JAY L. HALIO

In Memoriam: W. V. O'Connor

In the first O'Neill play ever produced, "Bound East for Cardiff," a dying seaman complains to his friend:

> *Yank.* This sailor life ain't much to cry about leavin'—just one ship after another, hard work, small pay, and bum grub; and when we get into port, just a drunk endin' up in a fight, and all your money gone, and then ship away again. Never meetin' no nice people; never gittin' outa sailortown, hardly, in any port; travelin' all over the world and never seein' none of it; without no one to care whether you're alive or dead. . . . There ain't much in all that that'd make yuh sory to lose it, Drisc.
> *Driscoll.* (gloomily) It's a hell av a life, the sea.
> *Yank.* (musingly) It must be great to stay on dry land all your life and have a farm with a house of your own with cows and pigs and chickens, 'way in the middle of the land where yuh'd never smell the sea or see a ship. It must be great to have a wife, and kids to play with at night after supper when your work was done. It must be great to have a home of your own, Drisc.

Yank's vision of "a home of your own" was never to be fulfilled, neither for Yank nor for most of the characters in O'Neill's long and

13

fruitful dramatic career launched that night in Provincetown in 1916. But the quest remained central to O'Neill's work, and the earnestness of this seeking as much as his indefatigable experimentation with technique greatly contributed to the revitalization of the American theater in the early decades of his century—even as one illusion of "home" after another was examined and found for what it was—an illusion.

In "The Long Voyage Home," the next play in the series *S. S. Glencairn*, the Swede Olson seems about to realize Yank's dream of settling down on a farm after years at sea. He has two years' pay saved to buy a farm, after he returns to his mother and brother in Stockholm. But although when he hits port he resolutely keeps off the drink that has wrecked all his previous dreams of returning home, Olson is yet a prey to the treachery of men like Fat Joe and the whore, Freda, who drug him, rob him, and then shanghai him aboard the notorious ship "Amindra." So poor Olson never makes it home. But what if he had? The answer lies in another play of the sea, really a kind of sequel to "The Long Voyage Home," if also a full-length play in its own right. Chris Christopherson, in *Anna Christie*, voices many of the same sentiments as Yank or Olson about a sailor's life and "dat ole davil, sea." Like Olson he has followed the sea, never—or seldom—getting back home, until his wife tires of waiting for him and leaves Sweden for relatives in Minnesota. When she dies, Chris decides to let their little daughter remain on the farm with her cousins so that she will never know a father like him or the life of the sea. But Chris's notion of a happy, healthy life on the farm is cruelly wrong: Anna's real history up to her arrival in New York to find him years later makes this point clear. Her cousins, hardly benevolent, have worked her to the marrow, seduced her, and generally treated her more like an animal than a human being, let alone kin. Ironically, it is at sea, aboard her father's barge, that Anna begins to find the peace of mind and harmony of spirit that restores her health and well-being. It is also at sea aboard the barge that she meets the shipwrecked sailor, Mat Burke, who comes out of the fog one night and recognizes the real strength and beauty that now stand revealed in her.

When Mat and Anna fall in love, Chris opposes their union: he wants something better for his daughter than anything that "dat ole davil sea" has spewed up for her. He fails to understand the changes in Anna, and what Mat can mean to her, partly because he is ignorant of her past and partly because he is deeply prejudiced:

he knows too well what being married to a sailor would be like. On her part, Anna loves Mat too much to marry him, being what she has been. It is not until she tells both Mat and Chris the truth about herself that any real union is possible, or that any reconciliation between the two men can occur.

But though the play seems to end happily, its last words strike again a note of gloom and foreboding, as Chris mutters: "Fog, fog, fog, all bloody time. You can't see vhere you vas going, no. Only dat ole davil, sea—she knows!" In this, and in the play's strong undercurrent of morbid fatalism, there is much to support O'Neill's own view that the ending is not really happy, that in it we can find little cause for genuine rejoicing over these poor souls, whose pasts will inevitably rise up to wreck their meager chances for happiness. Boy-gets-girl was not necessarily a happy outcome in O'Neill's opinion or in his experience, as another early play, *Beyond the Horizon*, bitterly demonstrates. The promise of a loving marriage may too often turn out to be just another illusion. Sacrificing his vision of freedom, of life over the rim of the hills that have imprisoned his spirit, Robert Mayo does so for the love of a girl who, he later discovers, cannot begin to match his dreams. Still, as the later—and greater—plays show, if there is any hope for man at all, if there is any "home" for him this side of the tomb, it is in the love of a generous-hearted woman, or someone who can help him find a faith in and beyond himself by which he may live. The quest for home thus becomes a quest for love and for conviction, but in O'Neill's work it is a quest that more often than not remains tragically unfulfilled.

Long Day's Journey into Night is not only, by common consent, the greatest of O'Neill's plays (and, ironically, one he never saw— or wished to see—produced in his lifetime); it is also the drama which most powerfully and autobiographically examines those forces which impel many of his other works. It is thus the central document of his dramatic career. Concerned with members of a single family, it explores within the compass of a single, critical day the pressures—and the causes of those pressures—which, despite the love each one feels for the others, compel them to drive one another to despair. The action takes place in August, 1912, at the summer home of the Tyrones. James Tyrone, a famous American actor (modeled on O'Neill's father, James O'Neill), has earned a fortune since the days when, as an Irish immigrant kid, he had to work in sweatshops to help support his mother and brothers and sisters. He has spent most of this money, however, on bad real estate investments, and the only thing he has to show for them is this summer home which, his wife Mary complains, is not a home at all. Most of the year they are on the road with the play that has made him famous but for which he has sacrificed what might otherwise have been a distinguished career as a Shakespearean actor. His Irish origins, his profession, the notoriety of his sons' behavior, and other causes have also combined to exclude the family from the genteel society that his wife knew before marriage and longs to return to, with ever diminishing hopes.

For Mary has never been able to fit in with her husband's professional friends, nor—unhappy and lonely though she remains —has she been able to break with the man she knows loves her and whom she also loves, despite his failure to provide the home that she so desperately wants and needs. This is her predicament, and it is seriously complicated by her feelings of guilt over the death of her infant son, Eugene, and the present illness of her youngest son, Edmund. Unable to find other solace, she relapses into the drug addiction that began with Edmund's painful birth and has helped ever since to shut her off from present painful realities.

As the play opens, it is a sunny, summer morning in what seems to be an ordinary family home. But it is not long before signs of mounting tension appear. For the last two months—or since her most recent return from a sanitorium—Mary has apparently been well enough to give her family the sense of "home" that they have also missed and that her sons Jamie and Edmund have come to regard as a priceless gift. But Edmund's wretched health, the fear that he may have consumption—the cause of her father's death—have already begun to revive feelings that she has hitherto found unbearable. Her wandering around sleeplessly the previous night, her growing nervousness, the beginnings of her withdrawal from normal relationships increasingly worry her husband and her sons, who now see (and not without feelings of guilt themselves) their hopes for a continuing, stable home badly threatened. As Mary resumes her drug-taking, their worst fears are realized, and they feel cruelly cheated by what they are now forced to consider a baseless illusion, a dream of happiness as hopeless as any of those of the past which make Mary their victim by the end of the play.

Mary's lapsing into drug addiction affects her family in other ways besides their sense of betrayal and deprivation. For James, her leaving them in this way brings doubts about the meaning of his own life and reduces him, finally, to a doubly defeated and broken old man. Trying to justify his mistakes—his surrender of nobler aspirations, his real estate ventures, his stinginess—he wonders now what it was he wanted to buy that could have been worth such sacrifice, and he can find no answer. For Jamie, the older son, his mother's breakdown causes him to break down also. Had she been able to keep off drugs, he feels he could have kept off his poison—the drinking, whoring, and bitter cynicism that now return to claim him. Edmund's situation is at once more desperate and more hopeful. Afflicted definitely by consumption, and worried that his father, superstitiously believing the disease is fatal, may send him to a cheap state hospital, Edmund is further tormented by the thought that his mother has forsaken him, too. But unlike Jamie, he has already begun to rely more and more upon himself and not upon any member of his family, no matter how dearly he loves and wants them. His years as a seaman, his more recent work as a reporter and poet are some evidence of this independence. Most of all, his experiences at sea have afforded a few glimpses into the possibility of joy and harmony in life and, even, a sense of "belonging."

Appropriately, Edmund describes this vision to his father late that night during a moment of unusual confidence between them. He tells of the time when, on an old square rigger bound for Buenos Aires, lying alone on the bowsprit in the moonlight, he "became drunk with the beauty and singing rhythm" of the ship and for a moment lost himself utterly.

> I was set free! I dissolved in the sea, became white sails and flying spray, became beauty and rhythm and became moonlight and the ship and the high dim-starred sky! I belonged, without past or future, within peace and unity and a wild joy, within something greater than my own life, or the life of Man, to Life itself! To God, if you want to put it that way.

Another time, aloft in the crow's nest of a steamship, he again knew the ecstasy and release, again experienced "the peace, the end of the quest, the last harbor, the joy of belonging to a fulfillment beyond men's lousy, pitiful, greedy fears and hopes and dreams!" These moments were, as Edmund realizes, comparable to "a saint's vision of beatitude," when the veil of things is suddenly drawn back.

> For a second you see—and seeing the secret, are the se-
> cret. For a second there is meaning! Then the hand lets
> the veil fall and you are alone, lost in the fog again, and
> you stumble on toward nowhere, for no good reason!

As against the usual experience of life's meaninglessness, its absurdity, these moments of mystic insight, of oneness and wholeness
and harmony, of man's being at home in the universe, stand out
sharply. The passage clearly links O'Neill to the great romantics,
such as Wordsworth, and against those with whom he is more generally associated and whom Edmund much enjoys reading or quoting: Nietzsche, Baudelaire, Strindberg. Edmund's visions, however,
are extremely brief—as brief as they are rare. The question becomes,
Are they powerful enough to sustain him or anyone else so beset
with ill health and loneliness and a strong sense of his own un-
worthiness and unwantedness?

The ending suggests a pretty definite negative, but for a more
complete answer it is necessary to move out of the play and into the
autobiographical matrix from which it emerged. As his various bi-
ographers have shown, O'Neill was beset by exactly these sorts of
obstacles. Like Edmund, he was "a stranger who never feels at
home. . . .who can never belong, who must always be a little in
love with death." What saved him from complete self-destruction
was undoubtedly his instinct for self-preservation coupled with an
essential toughness, but also the beginning of his commitment to
writing. Though the fictional Edmund regards himself as no true
poet and his inspired speech to his father as mere "stammering," the
"native eloquence of us fog people," the real O'Neill's devotion to
his art not only produced astonishing plays, but gave him a "home,"
a focus for his life such as no place or person—not even, perhaps,
his third wife Carlotta, who bears the glowing dedication of this
play—could ever provide him with for so long or so well. Such
gimpses as Edmund has had into the beautiful harmony of the
universe may otherwise be available, then, at least since the decline
of religion in the West, only in art (as E. M. Forster has said), in
the making of fictions, where man can create the kinds of unity and
coherence and, hence, meaningfulness that actual life insistently appears to deny.

Jamie Tyrone (like Jamie O'Neill) was not nearly so fortunate. As *A Moon for the Misbegotten* (the sequel to *Long Day's
Journey*) shows, he was far more closely and disastrously de-

pendent upon his mother's love and approval than was his younger
brother. His happiness lay entirely in her hands, as when years
later, after the elder James's death, he spent a few serene years with
her. At her death (by cancer), he is plunged into a profounder
despair than ever. He finds scant relief either from drink or from
the whores in whose arms he recites Dowson's "Cynara" before
awakening to a gray dawn creeping up from beyond dirt-smeared
windows. Only the Irish giantess, Josie Hogan, the daughter of his
father's old tenant (the "Shaughnessy" of *Long Day's Journey*),
gives him any real respite and comfort; for he correctly judges that
she is not the scandalous woman she persuades others she is, but a
virgin after all and as pure in body as she is in heart. It is to Josie
that he unfolds the harrowing tale of his drunkenness and debauch-
ery at his mother's death; and it is Josie who fully understands his
plight and her inability—much though she would like—to give
him anything more than an evening's moonlit rest, or a brighter
dawn to awaken in than others he has lately known. This much
expiation, and love, she can give him. It is not enough to redeem
him home—he is too lost in despair for that—but it is as much as
he can any longer bring himself to accept.

Strongly contrasting with Jamie's situation (or Jim, as he is now
called) is the healthier and sturdier relationship between Josie and
her father, Phil Hogan. Part of the plot deals with Hogan's concern
that his new landlord, Jim, may evict him to get a higher price for
his land. The threat is never more than a joke, but thematically it
serves to show how Josie and her father, devoted to each other in
a gruff, rough sort of way, are also devoted to their ramshackle old
farm and the kind of life they lead on it. Free of pretence—or at any
rate those pretensions of respectability and moral superiority represented, for example, by Harder, the Standard Oil magnate's
heir, or Josie's younger brother Mike—their life is both earthy and
genuine. It is this, besides the warmth and strength and beauty beneath Josie's grotesque appearance, that Jim sees and makes him
swear never to sell their farm to anyone else, whatever the offer
(and at one point Harder makes an exceptionally high one). Homeless himself, and in many ways corrupted or depraved, he nevertheless can cherish what Phil and Josie have and, for once, prevent
his destructive cynicism from wrecking that, too.

The temptation to wreck the little that others may have, out of a
sort of jealous revenge on life, is a very real one, as O'Neill demonstrates in another late play, *The Iceman Cometh.* It would seem

that the poor derelicts at Harry Hope's place had nothing much left to lose, that they had really come to the end of the road. As one of them, shrewd Larry Slade, describes Hope's joint to a new arrival, it is

> the No Chance Saloon. It's Bedrock Bay, The End of the Line Café! The Bottom of the Sea Rathskeller! Don't you notice the beautiful calm in the atmosphere? That's because it's the last harbor. No one here has to worry about where they're going next, because there is no farther they can go. It's a great comfort to them.

Slade, of course, is wrong. There is one more place they can go and, as Clifford Leech and others have shown, it is Hickey's function to bring them face to face with it. It is despair, posing in the disguise of intellectual honesty; and one of the ironies of the play is that until almost the very last, Hickey, the salesman, is himself unaware of what he is really selling or of the underlying motives for his behavior.

Hickey's basic error, or delusion, is that he can bring peace to Harry Hope's down-and-outers. He thinks that once they confront the truth about themselves—that there is no "tomorrow," that they are living in a world of pipe dreams—they will discover true spiritual contentment. He bases this conviction on his own experience, which, as it gradually is revealed, is as false as the wares he tries to sell the others.

For these down-and-outers are not so torn as Hickey tells them they are. True, they are incorrigible drunkards and has-beens: they drink mainly to forget their sordid present (and most of them succeed in this far better than Jamie Tyrone). Living in the hazy glow of their sentimental version of the past, they are hardly the pictures of mental anguish that Hickey, judging from his own domestic unhappiness, supposes they are. They have fought their battles with present reality, and lost; now they are at peace with their dreams—the peace that only pipe dreams provide for the defeated. However illusory or vain, these dreams still have the important saving grace of enabling these men to go on living, at no matter how low a level. Not until Hickey forces them to see themselves and their dreams for what they really are do anguish and strife develop: Captain Lewis and General Wetjoen bitterly quarrel and leave, as do Joe Mott (a Negro) and several others. Willie Oban struggles to take up his long abandoned law career, and Jimmy Cameron tries to retrieve his in journalism. Even Harry staggers out to take that "walk around the ward" he has been contemplating for years. But none can sustain the exposure and, welcoming defeat again, they all return to Hope's saloon.

And, for the moment, to Hickey. For their defeat is what Hickey, it seems, had privately predicted. As Tom Driver has shown in his essay, Hickey is the salesman not of redemption, but of death. His murder of his "dearly beloved wife" Evelyn clearly reveals this, along with his own cravings after death (he has already informed the police and is waiting for them to carry him off). His peace is death's peace, the final victory of despair. The others—all except Parrit, who commits suicide, and Slade, who is Hickey's "only real convert to death"—at least have the will to go on, however whiskey-sodden and dream-ridden their lives may be. And, together, they have a home, such as it is; and such as it is, home (as Robert Frost says) is where when you go there they have to take you in. Harry Hope always takes them in; for all his gruffness, he is glad to have them. For they make up his "home," too. The only home to which Hickey can look forward now is the illusion of a happier reunion with Evelyn after he is executed.

Never an optimist, O'Neill nevertheless allows a somewhat more uplifting conception of home to emerge in *A Touch of the Poet*. Like many of the sad derelicts in *The Iceman Cometh*, but endowed with much greater vitality, Con Melody lives off the dreams of past glory he won as a British officer at the Battle of Talavera. Much to his lasting chagrin, he has married the peasant girl, Nora, whom he made pregnant before going off to war, and they have a daughter, Sara. Driven from the army by scandal, he brings his family to America, but they find little happiness in their new home—a poorly paying tavern that Melody has bought outside of Boston. Unaccepting of his shanty Irish countrymen, and rejected in turn by wealthy Boston gentry, like the Harfords, Melody remains a proud, lonely outcast who enjoys quoting from *Childe Harold* and assuming other grandiloquent poses more appropriate to his military past than to his present situation.

When events concerning Sara's relationship with young Simon Harford conspire to smash Melody's illusions, he bravely destroys his handsome riding mare—the last vestige of his aristocratic past—and adopts the manner of the shanty Irish that he has loathed. But, as some critics have seen, Melody (like Hickey) simply trades one illusion for another, for he is no more like Patch Riley, Dan Roche, and the rest, than he is the Duke of Wellington or Simon Harford's father. Even Sara, usually so hostile to her father's pretensions, cannot bear this sudden change and pleads with him to resume his identity as "Major Melody." Only Nora, his wife, truly understands what is happening and can accept this transformation as she has long accepted her husband's mad posturing and disdain. What sustains her now as earlier is the "pride" of her love for him. It is different from the pride, or self-centeredness, that Sara shares with her father and that may prevent her, Nora suspects, from giving all of herself to Simon: which is what love is and which has saved Nora from the loneliness that has tormented Melody. It provides the necessary focus, a reason for being, and through it Nora achieves stature in the play. Eventually, after her own fulfillment with Simon, Sara comes to recognize this achievement:

> Sure, I've always known you're the sweetest woman in the world, Mother, but I never suspected you were a wise woman too, until I knew tonight the truth of what you said this morning, that a woman can forgive whatever the man she loves could do and still love him, because it was through him she found the love in herself; that, in one way, he doesn't count at all, because it's love, your own love, you love in him, and to keep that your pride will do anything.

Though superficially Nora, hard-working and long-suffering, seems scarcely better off than the derelicts and the tormented here or in O'Neill's other plays, her pride in love has enabled her more than to endure, but to be fulfilled. Nor is her fulfillment illusory. It looms as real and as large, let us say, as in another context Lena Grove's achievement looms both large and real in Faulkner's *Light in August*.

In *More Stately Mansions*, the sequel to *A Touch of the Poet*, Sara Melody stands in greater danger of forgetting what she has learned through her mother. The two plays are the only ones that survive of the great cycle that O'Neill began in the 30's but because of increasing illness could not complete. He called the cycle *A Tale of Possessors Self-Dispossessed*, and indeed the theme of the self-dispossessing power of greed is inherent in many of O'Neill's works. It obviously characterizes James Tyrone; but in subtler ways Mary and Jamie in *Long Day's Journey* also suffer the loss of their souls through their attempt to "possess," or their inability wholly to give. By giving of themselves, Josie Hogan and Nora Melody not only provide a haven for others, but possess their own souls in peace as well.

A haven for Simon Harford is what Sara sets out to provide, too. But even before their marriage, in *A Touch of the Poet* Sara reveals herself as motivated almost as much by her desire to overcome her shabby origins as an inn-keeper's daughter as by her sincere love for the Thoreauvian young man whom she takes for her husband. By the beginning of *More Stately Mansions,* Simon has already become a moderately successful businessman. Though Sara encourages him in his old dream of writing a Rousseauesque book "that will save the world and free men from the curse of greed in them" she does so chiefly to make him see the folly of his ideas. Thus the practical, ambitious side of Sara grows dominant. It is balanced, in Simon, by the romanticism that he inherits from his mother, Deborah Harford, who in this play assumes a role of major importance (she appears briefly in *A Touch of the Poet*). In fact, as the play unfolds, it takes on the structure of much older morality drama in which two angels struggle to gain the soul of a man.

O'Neill's morality pattern, however, is quite complex. The destructiveness of Deborah's fantasy world matches that of Sara's materialism, and both women, wife and mother, show qualities of love, devotion, and concern for Simon's well-being that are hardly to be condemned. The split in Simon's character is thus complicated by similar divisions in each of theirs, as all three develop the theme of "self-dispossession." But at the center remains Simon, who by the final act is in serious danger of being completely destroyed by this bifurcation in his life. Unity must be restored, or he will be utterly torn apart. Reconciliation of these opposing forces is no longer conceivable, for an earlier, artificial one succeeded only in isolating Simon in his own home from both wife and mother and in driving him harder than ever to the extremes of playing one off against the other. Now, these opposing forces appear so evenly matched, so equally strong, that not one reconcilement but victory of one over the other seems his only hope for survival.

These indeed are the terms in which Simon proposes the "final solution" to his anguish, as he prepares to choose between Sara and Deborah. But he is effectively deprived of his choice—to enter finally and irrevocably his mother's dream world—by the emergent heroism of both women, neither of whom wishes to see Simon destroyed by this extremity, but is willing to undergo destruction herself first. Significantly, Sara makes the initial gesture of self-sacrifice. However, just as Deborah has victory within her grasp, she renounces it, partly because she is too proud (and a little afraid) to see herself outdone in generosity by her rival, but also because her genuine love for her son triumphs at last. Hence she alone enters the summer house, the symbol of final surrender to fantasy, and emerges a few moments later more deranged than even Mary Tyrone at the end of *Long Day's Journey*. At the same time, Sara prepares to destroy the business empire which she has spurred Simon into building and which she knows is thoroughly rotten. She is now ready for a new life with him—or rather a resumption of one long ago discarded on the old farm where they began. Simon's book, which she now hopes he will write, may not save the world, but she realizes that it will surely save him. And by helping him, if only by loveing him in this selfless fashion, she will save herself and so free them both from the "curse of greed" that has marred their life together.

Reviewing O'Neill's accomplishment in the late plays, Professor Driver comments that "no character expresses the rejection of life so absolutely as Larry Slade, but each of those plays is written from his perspective." *More Stately Mansions* is not included in this estimate because it was not yet published, but I suspect that after reading it Professor Driver would not alter his view. This view strikes me as excessive, all the more because it curiously overlooks those aspects in the plays which Driver personally regards as important in his own philosophy as opposed to O'Neill's. He perhaps too readily associates the dramatist with the neo-Stoicism of nonreligious philosophers of existentialism, like Sartre and Camus, for whom courage and resignation are the essential virtues with which man can face the central fact of his existence—his despair in a world radically deprived of meaning. "If Paul Tillich is right," Driver continues,

> that the basic anxiety of our age comes from the threat of meaninglessness, it is not difficult to see that O'Neill offers a remedy for that anxiety. His plays declare that the meaning of life is its inevitable progression toward death. This is not, of course, an assertion which gives meaning to any of the particularities of life. In fact, it drains them of meaning. But it is a way of showing that its pattern is basically simple and imperturbable. The bleakest philosophy is preferable to chaos.

That O'Neill's philosophy is bleak, no one will deny; but that
it is as bleak as all this, requires some examination. Without wish-
ing to take unfair advantage by references to the one play Driver
could not consider (the same points could be made by citing others,
though not so obviously), let me quote part of Simon Harford's
speech near the end of Act III as he tries to convince his mother
that they should get rid of Sara:

> Our whole cowardly moral code about murder is but
> another example of the stupid insane compulsion of man's
> petty vanity to believe human lives are valuable, and re-
> lated to some God-inspired meaning. But the obvious fact
> is that their lives are without any meaning whatever—that
> human life is a silly disappointment, a liar's promise, a
> perpetual in-bankruptcy for debts we never contracted, a
> daily appointment with peace and happiness in which we
> wait day after day, hoping against hope, and when finally
> the bride or bridegroom cometh, we discover we are kiss-
> ing Death. . . . Or, obsessed by a fairy tale, we spend
> our lives searching for a magic door and a lost kingdom
> of peace. . . . And when we find it we stand and beg be-
> fore it. But the door is never opened. And at last we die
> and the starving scavenger hogs of life devour our carrion!

These embittered remarks would seem to confirm everything that
Professor Driver has said, except that while they brilliantly portray Simon's despair at this point, they do not represent either
O'Neill's total view or the play's. We may look in vain for any follow through of John Loving's religious conversion in *Days Without
End* (O'Neill's last play before his "late" period): no "God-in-
spired meaning" any longer emerges. But we do not look in vain
for such meanings as human beings like Sara eventually inspire or,
elsewhere, Josie Hogan, Nora Melody, and even Josie's father,
Phil. O'Neill had a touch of the romantic about him, as we saw in
Edmund's speech in *Long Day's Journey*. These other characters suggest that he had a touch of the humanist, too. What his philosophy
is specifically directed against is man's foolish longing for happiness on a more or less grandiose scale, as typified by James Tyrone's
faith in material security, or Jamie's and Simon's yearnings after
regressive reunion with their mothers. "Voyages" like those
end in disaster, as they must. But the fog and the night that cover
so much of men's journeyings are not altogether impenetrable. Cour-

age is certainly required, for much of life, as Simon complains, is without "security or faith or love but only danger and suspicion and devouring greed!" But not all of it. "The kingdom of peace and happiness in your story is love," Simon tells his mother, and it is; but it is not the love he desires from her or the kind that Sara has chiefly given him. Such love is indeed illusory or treacherous. Paradoxically, the door of the kingdom will never open while we stand and beg or insist or whine before it. It opens only when we have offered up the treasures of our own kingdom. So, out of the fog and the night, Mat Burke comes to Anna Christie; or, after years of belittling, Con Melody again kisses Nora's lips and her hair.

O'Neill thoroughly understood the paradox of the locked kingdom and its key, and he especially understood how difficult and often impossible it is for most human beings, given their limitations and the usual conditions of life, to find the key, or, finding it, to turn the lock and enter. This is the knowledge that he dramatizes in his plays and that saves many of them from gross sentimentality. I do not join those critics who find *Days Without End* the worst play O'Neill ever wrote (I have a harder time, I confess, with *Ah! Wilderness*); for I consider the struggle between John Loving's two selves to be more significant and important than the ending, which has come under so much fire. The struggle, for John as for Simon Harford, is a struggle to the death and not simply a pose. If something is gained at the end, it is gained with great difficulty and not without cost. And man does not always win, as we find in *Long Day's Journey;* indeed, he but rarely emerges a winner. In the earlier plays, such as the series *S. S. Glencairn* with which we began, responsibility for failure is often shifted from the individual to "fate," but later on in his career O'Neill probed more carefully and deeply the causes within man that lead to his undoing. Mary Tyrone may try to blame "life" for the misfortunes that have beset her, and she surely convinces herself, if not the others, like James, who is abler to see the botch of things he himself has made, and why. Nor does Edmund so entirely yield to the desperate cynicism that Mary's defeat arouses in his brother, Jamie.

Such considerations as these should redress the balance, but ought not to distort the undoubted emphasis of O'Neill's later plays upon the "hopelessness of hope" in which he conceived most of his characters or their predicaments. May not the same courage, however, that helps men to face their inevitable passage to death help them also to overcome the destructive forces in the world or in themselves? I doubt that O'Neill would have agreed to a proposition so baldly stated, but there is considerable evidence in his plays to suggest affirmation of this view. Or, to put it another way, O'Neill doubtless saw the possibility *as a possibility,* but for many reasons in his experience he was unable to endow that possibility with much hope. At the end of his own life, we know, he faced death with precisely those virtues of courage and resignation that Professor Driver describes. But by then he was no longer able to write, and the woman he had loved most and who so often had relieved his despair was nearly worn out and driven to we know not what extremes. The "home" that work and love had provided him, though more lasting than his other earthly homes, inevitably had to give way to illness and to death. But his plays remain as powerful testimonies to such homes as man may hope for in his otherwise drifting and meaningless existence.

Six Characters in Search of an Author and Desire Under the Elms:
What O'Neill Did Not Learn From Europe

by WILLIAM E. TAYLOR

An interesting question to ask about Pirandello's *Six Characters in Search of an Author* is this: why did the author not write the play for the six characters? We know that he had conceived of them, and that he was urged enough by the characters themselves to go ahead and finish his job. Nevertheless, he refused to do so.

Two answers are overtly advanced in the text of the play. One is that a play, once it is written and started on the road to production, is no longer the author's property. The Director says to the Father at one point of the action: "It's always a mistake to rehearse with the author present. He's never satisfied!" That gives us the picture from one perspective, that of the director. We can perhaps imagine the other perspective, that of the author, writhing as he watches director, scene designer, lighting technician, technical director and finally the actors, take and assume his realities and, if not misinterpret them, fail to interpret them as he had visualized them when he was creating their lives. As a matter of fact, something like this happens in *Six Characters* when the actors are trying to learn their parts from the characters. The Father protests to the Director: ". . . it is simply that they are not us." The Director answers: "Of course they're not! How can they be you if they're ac-

tors as well?" The Father tries lamely to explain: "It is that somehow . . . the play is becoming theirs. It isn't ours any longer." No one
can know what this means until he has a play of his own produced
by even the best-intentioned director and cast. The reality of the
play remains forever in the author's studio and in his mind.

A second reason why the author never wrote the play, according to the Stepdaughter, is that "he abandoned us out of de-
jection over the current condition of the theatre with its constant
pandering to public taste as measured by the box office. . . ." I suspect that no matter what age of the theatre is at issue, this statement would be relevant. It may, however, be more true in the twentieth century, and particularly in America, than in any other century and any other country.

Valid as these two reasons for not writing the play for the
Six Characters may be, however, I do not believe they are the real,
the final, reasons. To quote the Stepdaughter once more, when
she is describing how she pleaded with the author to write their play,
she says:

> I tried to tempt him, many times, when he was sitting
> at his desk at twilight, feeling a little melancholy, not even
> able to decide whether to turn on the lights or to let the
> shadows fill this room . . . and those shadows were filled
> with us, come to tempt him. . . . Ah, my life! My life!
> My life! What scenes we offered him! And I, I have
> tempted him more than all the others put together!

To answer why the author refused those scenes, that life, we
must go back to the play to see what is happening in it. The question that Pirandello raises, of course, is a venerable one: what is
reality? More particularly, however, he asks: what is the reality of
human character? His answer is the reason why John Gassner considers Pirandello one of the annihilators of modern drama, for Pirandello's answer is that human character or personality does not
exist at all. The Father presents the rationale for this idea when
he says:

> For me the whole drama lies in this one thing: that each
> of us believes himself to be a single person. It isn't true.
> With some people we are one person, with others we are
> quite a different person altogether. But to ourselves we re-
> tain the illusion of being always the same person to every-
> one. And we realize it isn't true when suddenly, to our hor-

ror, we are caught up into the air by some giant hook, frozen in time, suspended for all to see. Then we recognize that all of us was not in that particular action, that it would be an atrocious injustice to judge us by that action and that action alone. . . keeping us suspended in pillory, as if our life were made up of only that one moment.

A real person, then, is not a "single person" and is therefore not "true." A character, once *conceived,* however, *is* a single person, and therefore *is* true. The Mother says, for example:

Can't you see? It is happening now! It happens always! My torment is unending! I am always alive and subjected at every instant to torment which repeats itself over and over . . . I cannot even die. I must live it and feel it . . . forever.

Finally, Pirandello tells us what he is doing in what I call "the inversion scene" of the play, that point of the action when the characters are running through the prostitute episode and, by setting the stage to suggest Madam Pace's bordello, make Madam Pace, who is not yet present, actually appear. The Director and the actors think some kind of trick has been played on them, for, of course, they do not really understand what is happening at their rehearsal at all. But the Father understands it quite clearly. He says:

Stop it! Stop it, all of you! What you are seeing is truth itself! Why must you try to destroy it? Why must you call it a trick? This miracle of birth, this reality, called to life by the scene which we have just created, has more right to be here than any of you because it is more true! Which actress among you will play Madam Pace? Well, this is Madam Pace herself!

One is perhaps tempted to wonder why the Father cannot have the good grace of Prospero, accept the stage for what it is and agree to burn his book. But Pirandello was concerned with more than the inability of an actor to assume a role. He was really saying, I believe, that, philosophically, psychologically, existentially, a character is more true than a person. And he was, in this play, remorselessly carrying the logic of this premise to its conclusion. The true is the eternal moment of art. His thinking can be reduced to a syllogism:

Truth is art.
Reality is not art.
Reality is not truth.

This logic leads to a further conclusion: if truth is art, it is too horrible to bear, and this further conclusion leads to the attack on the Leviathan Aristotle. For, as the Director knows, the play that is to produce the reality (not the truth) of the characters must have a "recognition scene." It must be the scene between the Mother and the Son. It may be tragic, but it must lead to an enlightenment. What would the recognition scene be in a "play" in a "theatre . . . [that is] . . . pandering to the public taste as measured by the box office . . ."? Whatever the answer to that question might be, in the unwritten play as the characters enact it, there is no recognition scene. Instead, the son rushes out of the room to the garden, the little girl is drowned in the pool, and the little boy shoots himself. The stage directions for the scene that follows the shooting are as follows: *"there must be no doubt that the Boy is truly, in reality, dead."* And this is why the author did not write the play, because, to use another syllogism:

Art is Truth.
Truth is unbearable.
Art is unbearable.

My point here is this: Pirandello's play, *Six Characters in Search of an Author,* is a play of intellect. It is a play which probes the nature and the reality of drama, indeed of all art. It concludes that art is more true than reality. In being so, however, art shows us how horrible truth is—to the point that it is unbearable—and therefore it is possible to say that the artist is justified in not performing at all. In its relentless logic, *Six Characters in Search of an Author* carries us, and leaves us, at the still point of nothingness.

A massive power of intellect seems to be characteristic of modern European drama, from the relentless searching out and destroying of "idealisms" in Ibsen and Shaw; to the bleak naturalism of Strindberg, Hauptmann, and Gorki; to the nihilistic expressionism of Strindberg's *The Ghost Sonata* and *The Dream Play;* to the existential *nada y pues nada* of Sartre and Camus; to the absurdism of Ionesco and Beckett; to the apotheosis of inversion of Genet; to the subtle and grandiose theory of art as propoganda of Brecht. I am aware that not all European drama of this century is characterized by a total submision to the intellect; there are Lorca, Synge, Yeats, O'Casey, and perhaps Durrenmatt. But Durrenmatt's compatriot, and, I think, a more interesting writer, Max Frisch, for all his agonizing over what intellect and idealism have brought the world to, seems in *The Chinese Wall* to be saying we can no longer allow history to repeat itself, but history will repeat itself. In other words, he subjects his material to the careful scutiny of the intellect, he doesn't like what the intellect discovers, but he finds no other road to go for escape.

Eugene O'Neill, though he is the one American playwright to achieve international fame as a serious dramatist, nevertheless seems rather simple-minded after these writers. But O'Neill, too, has followed the hard-headed path of the intellectual down into the lower depths. Naturalism is the dominating mode of his earliest writings, and he never completely let go of it. In his early one-act plays, he is clearly using materials he has garnered from his own experiences at sea. His settings are already described in painstaking detail, though tinged with romantic overtones. His characters are drawn from life. His fables are stark, bitter in their fidelity to how life is—or to how life appeared to him at the time. And it appeared to him that man was caught in a trap from which there was no escape.

In the early one-act plays, there are the beginnings (incipient beginnings, admittedly) of his later experiments with expressionism. His sets, for example. No longer is the American theatre to have the panoramic backdrops of the *Great Divide* or *Madame Butterfly*. Instead, O'Neill describes his sets with great detail, as if he wants them to *work*, as if every smallest detail is important and contributes to the meaning of the play. In *The Moon of the Caribbees*, for example, the contrast between the naturalistic description of the deck of the ship and the background of coral beach, palm trees, and moonlight, seems to lift the setting beyond naturalism to expressionism. O'Neill's primary purpose, of course, is to create mood, and that is not expressionism. It is merely romantic. But when such a mood has a vital and integral relationship to what the play is about—to theme—it calls attention to itself not merely as place, or space, or time. It calls attention to itself as a distortion of these categories.

In *Moon of the Caribbees*, the appeal to the eye is reinforced by a second expressionistic technique which O'Neill was later frequently to experiment with, an appeal to the ear. The singing coming from the shore is more than merely romantic native music. O'Neill emphasizes it not only by his care in describing it but by contrasting it with the brassy song the sailors sing—"Blow the man down!"

—and by the jazzy music they dance to—"You Great Big Beautiful Doll!" At the end of the play, the shore music is described as follows: "There is silence for a second or so, broken only by the haunted, saddened voice of that brooding music, faint and far-off, *like the mood of the moonlight made audible.*" (Italics mine.) It seems clear that O'Neill wishes this to be more than merely romantic atmosphere. It takes on a reality of its own. Indeed, it is an attempt to *say* what none of his characters have the word for—what O'Neill himself does not have words for—not even through the cultivated and sensitive Smitty or the deep, if taciturn, Donkeyman.

The bells in *Bound East for Cardiff* function similarly as Yank nears his death.

It is interesting to note that, though character in the early one-act plays is drawn from O'Neill's personal experiences at sea, most of the major character-types he is to deal with later are already present. There is Paddy, who objects vigorously when he is actually called a hairy ape. There is Driscoll, the well-adjusted conformist, the William Brown who accepts life on its surface terms. There is the melancholy, brooding, aesthetic Smitty who is unable to find meaning or a place for himself in life, an early drawing of O'Neill's "defeated man," his Dion Anthony in *The Great God Brown,* Darrell in *Strange Interlude,* Eben Cabot in *Desire Under the Elms,* Larry Slade in *The Iceman Cometh,* and even the autobiographical hero of *Long Day's Journey Into Night.*

Of more particular interest to the present discussion, however, is the native woman Bella, an early hint of an idea O'Neill is to be obsessed with for the rest of his writing career, the earthy, uninhibited female type later to be symbolized under various guises as O'Neill's "God-the-Mother": the prostitute earth-goddess Cybel in *The Great God Brown,* and the frequent agonized allusions to God-the-Mother in *Strange Interlude.*

Bella, of course, is associated with the native music and so is the materialization of the call of the haunting, seductive, ever-present primal nature that sings like a siren from the shore out to the trapped, lonely men on the ship. O'Neill is to call this siren-song by many names in his later plays. It is to be heard in the insistent beat of the tom-toms in *The Emperor Jones,* the cry of Yank to "belong" in *The Hairy Ape,* Ella's death struggle with the Congo mask in *All God's Chillun;* it is associated not only with Cybel in *The Great God Brown* but with Dion Anthony's masked, sensitive cry that the meek shall inherit the earth. It is, in brief, the call of the heart, the call of what O'Neill came to call "God-the-Mother." And it is related to O'Neill's much-quoted statement that

> The playwright today must dig at the roots of the sickness of today as he feels it—the death of the old God and the failure of science and materialism to give any satisfying new one for the surviving primitive religious instinct to find a meaning for life in, and to comfort its fears of death with.

The anguish of O'Neill's search for meaning should not, of course, be minimized. His characters are obsessed with that anguish, with despair, to the point that he has been called by serious and knowledgeable critics a nihilist. And O'Neill sees man meeting doom; his typical hero is the "defeated man." As the O'Neill hero applies his intellect to the struggle of the sensitive man in a world of materialistic money-grubbers, or the clear-sighted man in a world of self-deceived illusionists, it is the former who inevitably is outnumbered and destroyed. This, O'Neill believed, was the only conclusion to be drawn from observation and experience. It might be said of him, as I have said of Pirandello, he concluded that "truth is unbearable."

But he could never conclude that "Art is unbearable." O'Neill simply was incapable of giving up. He was incapable of *believing* what he *knew*. To put it another way, in Lionel Trilling's words, "In short, O'Neill solves the problem of evil by making explicit what men have always found to be the essence of tragedy—the courageous affirmation of life in the face of individual defeat."

Perhaps I would be better off going back to *Six Characters,* where Pirandello, as a matter of fact, delineates the contrast I am trying to draw. The play which the actors expect to rehearse, Pirandello's *Rules of the Game,* is concerned with the conflict between intellect and passion. In the story of the six characters themselves, Pirandello pursues that theme, making the father representative of intellect and the Mother of passion. The Father dominates, and the catastrophe is total. There is no "tragic insight," no "tragic vision" in the classical sense, in the sense that Trilling has in mind when he says that "the essence of tragedy [is] the courageous affirmation of life in the face of individual defeat." Priandello is, of course, saying just the opposite. Though O'Neill reaches, intellectually, the same nothingness, he really cannot stand it. He never could, not from the beginning. His escape from

the trap of intellect is passion, and that passion is, in the last
analysis, the very essence of his work. It is remarkable that he was
so often able to get up off his knees and write the next play.

In *Desire Under the Elms*, Ephriam Cabot knows only the hard
rock of his God-the-Father. Eben Cabot, his youngest son, according
to the two older brothers, is the "dead spit'n image" of his father—
just as ambitious, just as hard, just as relentless; and Eben turns out
to be that, too. But there is another side to him. He is, according to
his father, according to Ephriam, "the dead spit'n image" of his
mother, who was soft, sensitive, and, ultimately, defeated.

Her ghost, however, haunts the house like the siren song haunting the deck of the *SS. Glencairn*. It is the earth-goddess again. And
when Eben and Abbie spend the night in the sanctuary of the sitting room that has been closed ever since Eben's mother's death, a
rather strange thing happens. Abbie, who, like Eben's mother, is a
sensitive person, full of the love of life, able to wax passionate and
almost mystical about the beauty of nature, exorcises, by taking the
place of, the haunting spirit. It is one of those grotesque scenes that
are always popping up in O'Neill, where his failure of language is
especially painful.

> Eben. She died. (*a pause*) Sometimes she used to sing
> fur me. (*He bursts into a fit of sobbing*)
>
> Abbie. (*both her arms around him—with wild pas-
> sion*) I'll sing fur ye! I'll die fur ye! (*In spite of
> her overwhelming desire for him, there is a sincere
> maternal love in her manner and voice—a horribly
> frank mixture of lust and mother love*) [*O'Neill is
> trying to create an image here for the meaning of the
> Virgin Mary, and he is falling flat on his face. The
> failure is magnificent! Had O'Neill been given the
> education of Gerard Manley Hopkins, there is no
> telling what he might have done.*] Don't cry, Eben!
> I'll take yer Maw's place! I'll be everythin' she was t'
> ye! Let me kiss ye, Eben!

The scene, of course, develops to a naturalistic mating in a "fierce,
bruising kiss," and it could be interpreted as merely the subtle and
understandable machinations of a sex-starved young woman married
to a man who is too old. But that would be seeing only the naturalism. That would be seeing only the intellect of the play, and the
painful language. O'Neill, I believe, really meant Abbie to become,

or to absorb, the ghost of Eben's mother and thereby embody the earth-goddess, the God-the-Mother principle. It is the "recognition scene" of the play, a scene which, in the logic of *Six Characters,* would not have happened.

And since the God-the-Mother principle is an irrational principle, when it comes to dominate Eben's life it leads to the errors of passion. Eben goes for the sheriff and turns Abbie in. Ephriam would, he says, do no such thing, but would stand by her and protect her. If, however, Eben's "mistake" leads to his defeat, it also leads to his victory—if you think that his returning, committing himself to prison with Abbie, and thereby affirming the validity and dignity of their love, is a victory.

In any case, it is not a victory of intellect; it is a victory of passion. It is the leap through the blank wall of nothingness to tragic affirmation; it is the victory of passion, of the call of the heart—to O'Neill the desperate, desperate call of the heart—over the *nada y pues nada* toward which the intellect kept driving him.

Clifford Odets: From Influence to Affluence

by R. BAIRD SHUMAN

Born in Philadephia in 1906, the young Odets received most of his education in the public schools of New York City where the family had moved during his childhood. His formal education ended when he was fourteen, but he was consumed by his overwhelming desire to become an actor. He became active in a neighborhood company called the Drawing-Room Players, graduated from this to Harry Kemp's Poets' Theatre, and in 1925 founded his own acting company composed largely of former associates from the Drawing-Room Company. This group presented sustaining shows on radio for some time. Finally Odets became part of a stock company and had a starring role in its production of *Abie's Irish Rose.*

During this entire period, Odets was learning valuable practical lessons about theatre; however, he realized that personally he was drifting. He was not spiritually or emotionally a part of the 20's; his dislocation led him to attempt suicide three times before he was twenty-five. Odets needed a cause with which to associate and identify himself, but he was not to find such a cause until the onset of the Depression provided it.

The social forces which were a part of the Depression era were vital to Odets in two ways, the most obvious of which was that they provided him with the raw material for writing the impassioned social dramas for which he has become most noted: *Waiting for Lefty, Awake and Sing!,* and *Paradise Lost.* As the social and economic impact of the Depression grew, Odets wrote like one possessed. He wrote with amazing speed; and his artistic instincts served him well, for some of his most admirable writing flowed from his pen almost automatically. *Waiting for Lefty,* for example, was the product of three nights of intensive writing in the Boston hotel room to which Odets nightly returned after working with the Group Theatre Company which was then doing the premier of Melvin Levy's *Gold Eagle Guy;* and the exceptionally vital and forceful arsonist scene in *Paradise Lost* was written late at night on the whitewashed wall of the author's room in the hotel at Ellenville, New York, where the Group Company was ensconced during the Fall of 1934. Odets, being without paper, could not stay his hand; and he captured the scene which sprang into his mind in the only way available to him.

The second impetus which came to Odets via the Depression was the founding of the Group Theatre in 1931. The Group, devoted to the Stanislavsky method of acting, was founded by Harold Clurman, Cheryl Crawford, and Lee Strasberg. It endeavored to offer actors some stability of income by giving them contracts for an entire season during which their dramatic talents would be employed in various ways. There was—at least ideally—no star system in the Group Theatre, and the Group was to function as a closely-knit company devoted to the encouragement of experimental theatre. Odets was a member of the Group Theatre from the very beginning, and his association with the organization continued until its final disintegration in 1941. The Group became family to Odets, and he made the greatest personal sacrifices of his life in order to preserve it when financial woes threatened its extinction. In order to enrich the strained treasury of the Group Theatre, Odets went to Hollywood in late 1935 and wrote for the films, an act which represented the most significant artistic compromise of his life. And in 1937, Odets, still under contract in Hollywood, wrote *Golden Boy,* his first patently commercial play, for the sole purpose of providing the Group with a stunning financial success.

Odets' devotion to the Group Theatre never flagged. Shortly before his death he told an interviewer that "without the Group Theatre I doubt that I would have become a playwright." Anyone who has read and studied Odets' work carefully can certainly verify the accuracy of this estimate. His early plays were written with the

Group philosophy firmly in mind; each of these plays was written for eight characters, six or seven of whom were essentially equal in dramatic importance. Odets' work as an actor with the Group Company made him especially attentive to the details of stagecraft which playwrights sometimes are unaware of or chose to ignore.

The early 30's produced a host of social dramatists, many of them associated with the Group theatre; however, the names of such people as Albert Bein, George Sklar, Paul and Claire Sifton, and Albert Maltz are now all but forgotten. Clifford Odets, on the other hand, continued until his death in 1963 to be active and somewhat influential in American theatre. The stereotyped, almost cliché themes that most social dramatists were dealing with during the Depression—the plight of the working man, pacificism, the decadence of American society, the evils of capitalism—often controlled the playwrights who were developing these themes; Odets, unlike most of the others, controlled the themes and wove them into the fabric of quality drama, producing as he did so a gallery of memorable and believable characters placed in easily identifiable and credible situations. While, like the others, he focused his creative attention upon social protest, he concerned himself more fully than most of his contemporaries were able to with causes rather than effects. Audiences left plays like *Waiting for Lefty, Awake and Sing!, Till the Day I Die, Paradise Lost,* and even *Golden Boy* grappling with real problems, determined to alter the causes that led to the problems which were pressing in on the common man of that period.

The play that first established Odets as a rising young playwright worthy of being closely watched by the critics and the public was the agitational-propaganda one-acter, *Waiting for Lefty.* The play was so timely and the theme at that time so cogent that vastly diverse audiences found themselves directly involved in the drama as it unfolded. Odets had set out to produce a play in the form of a minstrel show through which he was to present slice-of-life vignettes showing what effect a taxicab strike was having on a representative cross section of cab drivers, all hard pressed financially by the Depression. The form of the play could not have been better calculated to coincide with the temper of the times. As the various hack drivers, some of them well educated people who can find no other work, tell of their frustrations, the audience is gripped by a feeling that a social order which brings about such frustrations must give way to something better. And in the final scene when the murder of the union organizer is revealed and Agate turns to the audience and asks, "Well, what's the answer?" There can be only one response: the audience as a whole chants, *"STRIKE, STRIKE, STRIKE!!!"*

Here more than in any of his other plays, Odets builds his audience to such an emotional pitch that he is in a position to take unfair advantage of them. In order to achieve the advantage here as in most of his other plays, Odets juxtaposes the little man (who represents good) to the capitalist (evil). The little man is principled, wholesome, almost wholly appealing. The capitalist, who never appears on stage, thus implying that he is remote and disinterested, is allowed no redeeming qualities. However, to point this out is perhaps critically unfair just as it is critically unfair to say that *Rocket to the Moon* is a play which chronicles the amours of a rather dull dentist and his secretary. Odets was consciously writing allegory during most of his career, and allegory generally achieves its impact primarily through the presentation of extremes from a notable partisan viewpoint. *Waiting for Lefty* is concerned with exploring the inroads which poverty and uncertainty make upon human existence and notably upon family life; *Rocket to the Moon* is broadly about the theme of love in modern America. The particulars are selected essentially for their ability to promote the theme with which the writer is grappling.

Odets' concern with the family as a social unit has often been considered on purely literal grounds. However, its allegorical significance is of the utmost importance and must be considered by anyone who would understand and appreciate the impact of what is being said especially in such plays as *Awake and Sing!, Paradise Lost,* and *The Flowering Peach.* In *Awake and Sing!* particularly, the family becomes a sustained symbol of the family of nations or more broadly of the family of conflicting political ideologies. Three generations of the Berger family live together in considerable disharmony, pressed hard by the economic uncertainties of the Depression and made tense by the very physical proximity in which they must exist in their Bronx apartment.

The three members of the Berger family who carry the ideological substance and import of the play are Jacob, the somewhat disenchanted visionary and Marxist, who represents the older generation and ultimately commits suicide; Bessie Berger, the mother who must take care of the practical necessities which have to be attended to if the family is to live through the difficulties of the period; and her son, Ralph, who shares his grandfather's Marxist views and who is able to find neither security nor fulfilment in life because of the

socio-economic milieu into which he has plunged. As the action unfolds, one might tend to sympathize with Bessie, the mother, who
struggles valiently to keep her family together. But one must also
sympathize, perhaps more fully, with Jacob when, in his disgust
at Bessie's manipulation of her family, he says, "Marx said it—
abolish such families."

Bessie and her father are at opposite poles as are Bessie and
her son. Bessie's most telling line in the play is "I like my house to
look respectable." She will go to any extreme, violate any moral code
to achieve the appearance of respectability. The grossest example of
this determination on her part comes when she arranges to marry
her pregnant daughter to the unsuspecting and gullible Sam
Feinschreiber. Quite on the other hand is Jacob's pervasive statement, "Life should have some dignity." The irony is that Bessie, the
materialist, is also the activist. Jacob, the idealist, lives in his
world of thought, alone and passive. Odets' implication is obvious:
The strong shall inherit and subsequently destroy the earth for the
idealists who will serve as the fodder upon which the practical
materialists shall glut themselves.

By the time he wrote *Paradise Lost,* Odets had shifted his
focus considerably. He was writing now about the middle class
which, through the broad inroads the Depression was making upon
its economic security, was threatened with extinction. And in this
play, there are no answers, just unresolved dilemmas. Reading beyond and beneath the literal level, one finds Odets saying that the
only hope for the sympathetic protagonist, Leo Gordon, is that he,
as opposed to Sam Katz, his disreputable business partner, has children through whom he is presumably perpetuated. However, his
daughter Pearl is resigned to going through life unmarried, his son
Julie is dying of encephalitis, and his other son, Ben, is killed by
police bullets while committing a robbery. Hence there really appears
to be no more future for Leo than for Sam Katz.

It was not until 1954 in his redaction of the Noah story, *The
Flowering Peach,* that Odets used the family as an intrinsically unifying and hopeful social force. The emphasis in *The Flowering Peach*
is on rebirth and fertility. The generations have their misunder-
standings; but the disaster, the flood, gives them familial cohesion
and solidarity, whereas the disaster in the two earlier plays, the De-
presssion, was in essence divisive and destructive to the families
involved. *The Flowering Peach,* which is probably Odets' most
artistically conscious published play, on the one hand deals literally

with a situation sufficiently removed in time to permit both the author and audiences to view it with an objectivity which was not generally possible in *Awake and Sing!* or in *Paradise Lost*. On the other hand, being an allegory based on yet another allegory, *The Flowering Peach* departs from the stunning realism which on one level gave strength to the author's Depression plays, but also led to serious misreading of them by critics and audiences.

Odets' life reached a significant turning point in 1941, and his work was to show the marked effects of this turning. In this year the Group Theatre was finally dissolved, producing as its last play Odets' *Clash by Night*. Few of the old members of the company were still around; even Harold Clurman, Odets' staunchest friend and most faithful advocate, had departed for Hollywood. The production of *Clash by Night*, begun as a Group Theatre production, finally was backed by Billy Rose and was never fully identified with the Group Theatre.

In the same year, Odets and his actress wife, Luise Rainer, were divorced. The best word to describe Odets' state as he witnessed the decline and eventual end of both the Group Theatre and his marriage is "dissolution." The three plays which are generally thought to be a part of this period, the beginning of which was marked by Odets' going to Hollywood and being for some time removed from the Group, are *Rocket to the Moon* (1938), *Night Music* (1940), and *Clash by Night* (1941). Each of these plays is vitally concerned with love and with problems of identity. *Night Music* is especially strong in capturing the loneliness, restlessness, and quiet desperation which gripped people in our country as the Depression began to fade and the looming specter of war overshadowed the country. Less successful artistically is *Rocket to the Moon,* a play in which Odets personally had faith until his dying day. He contended that the play was ". . . about love in America, about the search for love, and all the things it turned out to be." However, the play was so lacking in the sorts of universals with which audiences can identify that the allegory which the author intended dissolves into banality, triviality, and rather maudlin sentimentality. The play is stunningly realistic, but the subject treated might better have been handled with a mixture of realism and romanticism such as that found in *Night Music*.

In *Clash by Night* are found strains of Odets' early social concern intermixed with his interest in the love triangle. The determinants in *Clash by Night* are essentially economic; and the play, although it was not successful either commercially or artistically, is not without distinctly commendable qualities. The character portrayal is very strong, especially that of the minor characters. Mr. Wilenski, an old immigrant who plays his violin in bars for drinks, is an unforgettable character in many ways suggestive of but stronger than Jacob in *Awake and Sing!* The major flaw in *Clash by Night* is that the homicide at its end is too sensational and is not fully motivated. The same sort of unrestraint that detracted from some of his earlier plays, most notably *Till the Day I Die* in which a Nazi Storm Trooper smashes the hand of the protagonist, remains a significant artistic problem in the ending of *Clash by Night*.

With the production of *Clash by Night,* which almost coincided with the entry of the United States into World War II, Odets withdrew somewhat from Broadway. He settled down in Hollywood and wrote a number of scenarios. He was not to produce another play until 1948 when *The Big Knife,* a bitter satirical diatribe about Hollywood, was produced on Broadway. This play was written with a sure hand and its forward thrust is great. The dialogue is crisp and the characters are well-defined. Marcus Hoff, the prototypical Hollywood film mogul who must always feed gluttonously on the talents of others, is drawn relentlessly as is Patty Benedict, the film columnist who can make and break careers according to her whim. The protagonist's agent, Nat Danziger, is described by the protagonist with typical Odets realism and economy: "Why did I ever add this burden to that grotesque, devoted soul? Did you ever notice? His lips move when he reads." But *The Big Knife,* technically strong though much of it is, does not end satisfactorily or credibly: Charlie Castle, the great film star who has just been blackmailed into signing a multi-million dollar film contract, commits suicide for very shallow and extrinisic reasons; one finds it difficult to be convinced that the ending is sequential with the rest of the play.

The ending of *The Country Girl* (1950) is much more plausible, and this play represents an artistic advance for Odets. The problem of the love triangle enters into the action, but the major question of the play is one of human interdependence and interrelation. Georgia, the young wife of Frank Elgin, a faltering, elderly, alcoholic actor, is trying to provide her husband with the sort of psychological support he needs when he has the opportunity to make a new start in the theatre. However, her good intentions are somewhat undermined when Bernie Dodd, the director of the play in which Frank is to make his comeback, becomes a threat to the Elgin marriage. However, Odets resolves the situation skillfully: he does not leave the audience with the probably unrealistic impression that Frank and Georgia will work out their difficulties, which are monumental. Rather, he permits Bernie to go off leaving the path clear for a possible resolution of the Elgins' problems. The audience must make its own decision about the final outcome. *The Country Girl* is trenchant and represents a new literary maturity for Odets.

The last of Odets' plays to reach Broadway was the warm and touching version of the Noah story, *The Flowering Peach* (1954). This play, for which Odets very nearly was awarded what would have been his only Pulitzer Prize, was not a rousing commercial success; however, it represents a considerable mellowing on the author's part while it maintains much of the integral social criticism of the earlier plays. One wonders whether history might not record this play as Odets' most significant dramatic work. In it one finds a careful balance, fully maintained throughout the play, of family bickering and family love, of wit and a painful grappling with quintessential social and philosophical questions. The resolution, which is traditional, is more satisfying than that in many of Odets' plays.

Odets, a notable innovator and a clear, forceful social commentator, will probably be longest remembered for his biting and credible dialogue sometimes verging on the poetic, from which such later writers as Tennessee Williams, Arthur Miller, and William Inge learned profitable lessons. His insights into the plight of the impoverished drew him close to a whole generation of men-in-the-street, and his unflaggingly realistic portrayal of the society which created the plight will probably assure his position as one of the most significant and positive forces in the emerging American drama of the 30's.

Maxwell Anderson: Traditionalist in a Theatre of Change

by WILLIAM E. TAYLOR

Maxwell Anderson, who also came to prominence in the 30's, began his career in the theater in the early 20's. His first play, *White Desert*, a verse drama, was produced in 1923, failed, and is not now in print. His second play, *What Price Glory?*, written in collaboration with Lawrence Stallings, was an enormous success and is now looked upon as one of the most significant breakthroughs of realism in American theatrical history. It is the first American play to treat war for what it is rather than as the background for chivalrous sentiments about heroism. In the second act (written, incidentally, by Stallings, not Anderson, who wrote the first and third acts), the scene is an embattled bunker on the Western Front and the atmosphere is drenched in terror, agony, and blood. Nevertheless, there is still something of a musical comedy atmosphere in *What Price Glory?* Captain Flagg and Sergeant Quirt are professional soldiers. They are tough as nails, they do their job well, and they take pride in it. The only suggestion of the Anderson philosophy later to be expressed in plays like *Mary of Scotland, Valley Forge,* and *Winterset,* is in the attitude of Flagg toward the high command and the politicians far behind the lines. Anderson was a pacifist and, as Harold Clurman calls him, a "quiescent anarchist" to whom all politicians and politician-generals were oppor-

47

tunists and exploiters of the common man. His Captain Flagg, in good-natured cynicism, says as much, using the colorful and forceful language of the American Marine.

Nevertheless, chronologically speaking, Anderson is a playwright of the 30's. His first successful verse play, *Elizabeth the Queen,* was produced in 1930. *Mary of Scotland* came in 1933. *Valley Forge* appeared a year later in 1934, and the play which most critics consider his most significant accomplishment, *Winterset,* was the first play to be awarded the prize of the New York Drama Critics' Circle. It appeared the same year as Clifford Odets' *Waiting for Lefty, Till the Day I Die, Awake and Sing,* and *Paradise Lost.* Though there is a good deal of social awareness in the plays of Maxwell Anderson, and though he likes the fruits of materialism and the exploitation of the weak by the strong as little as any playwright of the 30's, his political philosophy and his hopes for the future are based on an entirely different concept of the nature of man and man's social and political institutions from those of the more revolutionary Marxians who were his contemporaries.

As Harold Clurman has pointed out, Anderson is something of an intellectual. There is a *tentative* quality in the tone of his best plays that suggests the scholar's tendency to hesitate in the face of generalizations, even to suspend judgment between conflicting alternatives. This is not to say that he does not have a passionate belief in the dignity of man. His faith in man is as strong as that of Odets—stronger than that of Elmer Rice; there are no Mr. Zero's in the plays of Maxwell Anderson. Yet where Odets cries out that life should have a value not printed on dollar bills and that the solution is to "Strike! Strike!" because "No man fights alone," Maxwell Anderson offers no programs for salvation, no economics of the body and the soul, no politics for eradicating corruption.

His characters do talk, however; they often talk well and even subtly. The basic conflict in *Elizabeth the Queen* elicits what Shaw might call "the passion of discussion." Essex, the Queen's lover, has raised a rebellion against her. At her promise that she will share her kingdom with him, he disbands his army and turns the power back to her. She thereupon throws him into the tower to be executed as a traitor—hoping he will send her a ring she has given to him as a token that he will be granted forgiveness should he ever need it. At the eleventh hour, Essex has not sent the ring. In despair, Elizabeth sends for him and asks why. In one of the most effective scenes Anderson ever wrote, Essex and Elizabeth confront one another and their problem. She loves him, but loves her kingdom more. He loves her, but knows that his ambitious and hot-headed impatience with Elizabeth's cautious foreign policy would never allow him to resist attempting to wrest the throne from her. They talk this over, offering each other alternatives, but both know and recognize the irreconcilable nature of the paradox. So Essex finally leaves for the Tower and his execution. It is a scene worthy of Shaw—or, perhaps more correctly, of Shaw's own great exemplar, the Ibsen of *The Doll's House.*

There is action here, of course. Elizabeth at the last moment, as Essex is going out the door, cries out, "Take my kingdom!" But he keeps going and the play ends with a full view of Elizabeth's striken face. Anderson, however, leaves his audience with the impression that there is nothing that either Elizabeth or Essex can do. He will therefore go to his death, and she will live on through a powerful reign but a personally sterile life.

Such an ambiguous ending would be impossible in a play by Odets. In *Till the Day I Die,* which tells of the struggle and sacrifice of the Communist underground in Nazi Germany, there is at least the dignity of suicide for the protagonist, Earnest, and with the full knowledge that his comrades know him innocent of the charges trumped up against him by the Nazis. Further, "the cause" is still being championed, and though he dies, Earnest knows that his work will be a vital part of the ultimate victory.

Further, in *Awake and Sing,* Ralphie gives away the inheritance his grandfather had committed suicide in order to give him so he could be liberated from the squalor and debilitating atmosphere of a New York tenement district. Nevertheless, Ralphie faces the future with hope in his new-found determination to make the world over into something better.

In *Golden Boy,* Joe Bonaparte kills himself and Lorna Moon by driving his Deuzenberg madly through the night, but we know it is because he chose to write his destiny on dollar bills and newspaper headlines rather than fight social injustice with his strike-organizing brother, who, it is clear, has found personal integrity in his life and his work.

In Maxwell Anderson's plays, on the other hand, men do fight very much alone—and they fight a losing battle. As Elizabeth says, recognizing that Essex's enemies have been too clever, too unscrupulous, for him: "The rats inherit the earth." Anderson cannot believe that fallible men could ever bring about the millenium. He is convinced, rather, as he has General Washington say in the noblest of his plays, *Valley Forge,* "Men are mostly fools, as you are well aware. They'll govern themselves like fools. There are probably more fools to the square inch in the Continental Congress than in the Continental Army, and the percentage runs high in both." In *Winterset,* Judge Gaunt, characterized as an idealistic representative of democratic justice, has sent an innocent victim to his death as a result of political influence and public hysteria.

Anderson does not even seem to put much faith in history as a final arbiter of truth and justice. In *Winterset,* Mio has devoted all of his nineteen years to proving his father's innocence. His one burning ambition is to hurl the lie of his father's execution into the teeth of the neighbors who have forced him to leave his home in shame. The time finally comes when he has the proof he has sought and can publish it to the world, but when he discovers that the price of this victory is the life of the brother of Miriamne, his new-found love, he loses his taste for publishing the truth. He leaves his father's reputation where it had been given to him, in a pit of lime.

In *Mary of Scotland,* the theme of History as a court of last resort is even more explicit. The heroine at the end has lost everything. This time the chief rat to inherit the earth is Queen Elizabeth herself, who has carefully and brutally connived Mary's tragedy. First, Mary loses her lover, then her reputation, then her kingdom, and finally, at the end of the play, she sits alone in a prison in England, her personal freedom lost. Elizabeth offers Mary her liberty back if she will abdicate the throne of Scotland, and with it both her succession to the throne of England and her love for Bothwell. Mary refuses, justifying her actions by declaring that History will eventually be in her favor. Elizabeth replies,

> Child, child, are you gulled
> By what men write in histories, this or that
> And never true? I am careful of my name
> As you are, for this day and longer. It's
>   not what happens
> That matters, no, not even what happens
>   that's true,
> But what men believe to have happened.
>   They will believe
> The worst of you, the best of me, and that
> Will be true of you and me. I have seen
>   to this.

When Mary protests, Elizabeth says that history has already been written; she has letters to prove it. But, Mary objects, the letters are forged. What difference, asks Elizabeth. "All history," she says, "is forged."

"You would do this?" Mary asks.
"It is already done," Elizabeth answers.

In *Valley Forge*, Anderson turns to debunking popular concepts of the American past. Washington, fighting what seems a totally hopeless cause, discovers that there is a strong movement in the Continental Congress to make peace with General Howe without notifying their commander in the field. Washington interviews two representatives of the Congress at his headquarters and is told the following:

> This war began to protest our trade. The merchants are being run out of business by subsidies to English boats! It cut so deep in Boston there was no more profit in smuggling—and all our trade was smuggling, anyway! They dumped the tea in Boston harbor, and raised a hue and cry of "Freedom!" "Down with the tyrant!" Christ, what they wanted was profits, not freedom. But then the inland boys took up the yell, and ran together in mobs, and old Sam Adams made speeches, and cock-a-hoop, hell-bent, pell-mell made it spread to Virginia, and a pack of oyster-faced back-woodsmen met and signed a declaration, and then we were in trouble! Where's our trade now? Nobody makes money—not even the money-lenders. Nobody but the god-damn farmers selling pork to the British commissary! It's time to stop it! We've got to settle down and live, that's all, and why not under King George? If you fire-eaters can't make a living in time of peace, why, hell, the rest can't make one now!

"This sentiment prevails in Congress?" Washington asks. "It does, or it will shortly," he is told. So much for History as a court of final appeal in Anderson's world.

Finally, Anderson's protagonists find little comfort in religion, and here he seems to be in agreement with the general iconoclasm of the 30's. Mary of Scotland is Catholic, and she sets up an alter in her palace. She also speaks of God's spies revealing the truth when Elizabeth threatens her with a man-created history, but neither of these facts carries dramatic authority in the play. Elizabeth's argument crushes Mary, who finds consolation not in religion, but, as we shall see later, in a more humanistic argument. As for the fact of Mary's Catholicism, it functions as a source of conflict between Mary and most of her subjects, as well as between Mary and her lover, Bothwell. It provides Anderson, as a matter of fact, with another institution to deflate in the person of John Knox, whom he pictures as a thoroughly unpleasant, intolerant, even sadistic, egomaniac who employs all the forces of superstition and persecution to destroy Mary—the Whore of Babylon, as he calls her.

In *Winterset,* the religious tone is agnostic, a view which, I think, characterized Anderson's own belief. When Mio finally discovers the truth of his father's innocence, he exults—

> Now I could almost wish
> there was a god somewhere—I could almost think
> there was a god—and he somehow brought me here
> and set you down before me here in the rain
> where I could wring this out of you!

Later, when he knows that to tell the truth of his father's innocence will destroy Garth, his lover's brother, he laments—

> The bright, ironical gods!
> What fun they have in heaven! When a man
> prays hard
> for any gift, they give it, and then one more
> to boot that makes it useless.

To put it briefly, the idea of religion—of God as a solution to the human predicament—was an open question to Anderson. It is interesting to make comparisons here. With a writer like Odets, for example, the question of divine providence is irrelevant. What is relevant to Odets is social action. To Eugene O'Neill, the question was not only relevant; it was critical. *The Great God Brown,* for example, even more obviously then *The Hairy Ape* or *The Iceman Cometh*, is *about* man's quest for God.

Anderson fits in between these two views, that of Odets and that of O'Neill. The religious question is relevant because his characters take it seriously. They are puzzled, frustrated, even anguished over it. But it is not crucial in the sense that it was crucial to O'Neill. One is tempted to say, rather, that it was a *dramatic* issue with Anderson. Indeed, it would seem that rather than speak of the religious theme in his plays, it would be more correct to speak of An-

derson's religion of the theater, for this is precisely what Anderson
had. "In brief," he has himself said (In *Off Broadway*, pp. 33-34),
"I have found my religion in the theater, where I least expected to
find it, and where few will credit that it exists." He goes on to say
that

> . . . . the theater is the central artistic symbol of the struggle
> of good and evil within men. The teaching is that the
> struggle is eternal and unremitting, that the forces which
> tend to drag men down are always present, always ready to
> attack, that the forces which make for good cannot sleep
> through a night without danger . . . . It affirms that the
> good and evil in man are the good and evil of evolution,
> that men have within themselves the beasts from which
> they emerge and the good toward which they climb.

I think it is significant that Anderson should have put the
case in those terms. Scholarly though he was by temperament, he
was preeminently a man of the theater, a man of the stage, of
grease paint and footlights, of first-night audiences and newspaper
critics who rush away from their seats on the aisle to write reviews
that announce a hit show or an economic disaster. For twenty-
five years he wrote plays that met the test by fire of whatever the
public audience of the American theater may be. He had his successes and his failures, but there in the theater his life was, and
there was his religion, too.

What, we may ask, was this religion, on what creed did it
stand? Anderson has been accused by more than one critic of
pessimism. This is really the essence of Harold Clurman's summary
statement of Anderson's quality:

> The essence of Maxwell Anderson's work is a benevolent
> indecision. He is a quiescent anarchist. No man or govern-
> ment, he feels, is truly just; we all walk in a painful,
> glamorous maze. Life, as one of H. G. Wells' cockneys
> would say, is a rum go. Thus all problems are treated with
> a kind of soft skepticism and considerable affection. The
> tonality of the Anderson plays usually is composed of a
> gentle and slightly melancholy moodiness. Factorally and
> intellectually, all concrete considerations tend to lose their
> shape and to dissolve in a sad and tender blur with a never
> altogether extinguishable Puritan Christianity dominant.

> (*Lies Like Truth*, pp. 33-34)

This statement, it seems to me, is very nearly true. It would be hard to resist making the point, however, that Anderson's apparent belief in the fallibility of human nature, his lack of faith, as a corollary, in human institutions—political, economic, social, religious— his despair of history, even, which suggests the idea in Orwell's 1984, his belief, in the last analysis, that public truth as the subject matter of history is not necessarily Truth, his religious agnosticism —it would be hard to resist making the point that Anderson's concern with these matters is at least an affirmation of his belief in their value and the necessity for the dramatist to repeat this belief over and over again in the market-place. He may not have faith that man is good, that truth will prevail, that god is in his heaven watching every sparrow that falls; but he insists that these are the issues that men must keep before them and be concerned with.

But there is even more that can be said about Anderson's religion of the theater. In the first place, and almost to a fault, he believes intensely in the validity of love between a man and a woman. And in his best plays this romantic love has the power to redeem his lost protagonists. Elizabeth and Essex, Mary and Bothwell, Mio and Mariamne—star-crossed lovers all—are forced by their failures to commit themselves to one another; they learn thereby the lesson of sacrifice and self denial; and they emerge seared but nobler human beings as a result. This was not a popular idea with playwrights of the 20's and 30's, nor, for that matter, is it a popular idea with playwrights of the 50's and the present decade. It was, and is, far more the fashion to see romantic love as either an anachronism, as in *They Knew What They Wanted,* or as a kind of instinctive, animalistic game, as in *What Price Glory?* Furthermore, his lovers have certain qualities in common: the woman, fidelity, passionate faith not only in her man but in the transcendent nature of her love; the man, positive character, "strength of conviction not shaken by opposition." These are qualities "for which," Anderson says, "the race has a special liking on the stage." (*Off Broadway,* p. 26) He convinces us that he has a special liking for them in the race, and the implication is that they are universals, archetypes of "the god in man." They lead, of course, to lively theater, too. Anderson's heroes and heroines, as Clurman says, are always capable of "great gesture" and "splended duds."

Where this passionate belief in romantic love becomes a fault is in *Winterset,* where the love between Mariamne and Mio seems a little sudden. In *Elizabeth the Queen,* the romance is part of the *donné.* It is understood at the beginning of the action and given the audience in the exposition. In *Mary of Scotland* it is worked into the plot and develops out of the relationship between the two characters. But in *Winterset* it simply happens, with little preparation and no dramatic development. Anderson probably expected his audience to make the association of his nineteen-year-old Mio and his fifteen-year-old Miriamne with Shakespeare's Romeo and Juliet, but this association can hardly be called dramatic motivation. Furthermore, this love-at-first-sight changes the whole relationship between theme and action in the play. Up until the love-at-first-sight we have a young man burning to avenge his father's ghost, and until the last speech of the second act, this is what he is going to do. But in the third act—a rather short one—Miriamne commits suicide and expires on the dead body of her lover—he having suddenly learned forgiveness through his love for her.

A second positive value in Anderson's religion of the theater is his conviction that his heroes, though they will ultimately be destroyed by the rats who will inherit the earth, earn a triumph-in-defeat that reasserts their own dignity as well as the dignity of the human race.

In *Mary of Scotland,* for instance, Mary has the final word, not Elizabeth. She faces solitary confinement until her death or until her madness, yet she can say to Elizabeth,

> And still I win . . . .
>   In myself
> I know you to be an eater of dust. Leave me here
> And set me lower each year, as you
>   promise,
> Till the last is an oubliette, and my name
>   inscribed
> On the four winds. Still, STILL I win! I have been
> A woman, and I have loved as a woman loves,
> Lost as a woman loses. I have borne a son . . . .

The thematic justification for the references to Mary's son is that Elizabeth gave up marriage, according to the logic of the play, in order to rule England without the complications and distractions of intimate human relationships. Mary's son, therefore, is a symbol of her own humanity, the humanity Elizabeth has foresworn. There is, therefore, a kind of triumph in her final words to Elizabeth:

> My pride is stronger than yours, and my
>   heart beats blood
> Such as yours has never known. And in
>   this dungeon,
> I win here, alone . . . .
> I thank you for all kindness.

Much the same occurs in *Valley Forge* where Washington, betrayed by the Continental Congress, by many of his own generals, deserted by most of his soldiers—those he has left, ragged, starving, ill-equipped, and wounded—continues to fight the Revolution. Political liberty he holds to be a great ideal, but he has no illusions about it:

> When you deal with a king you deal with one fool, knave, madman, or whatever he may be. When you deal with a congress you deal with a conglomerate of fools, knaves, madmen and honest legislators, all pulling different directions and shouting each other down. So far the knaves and fools seem to have it . . . . I hope and pray it will get better. But whether it gets better or worse it's your own, by God, and you can do what you please with it.

Finally, Mio and Miriamne, perhaps the best examples of all, achieve victory in defeat when Mio renounces revenge for love.

The third value in Anderson's "religion of the theatre" is poetry. Anderson devoted his life to attempting to restore poetic drama to the modern stage, feeling it was the only right instrument to lift drama to the high function he believed it had. In an essay "Poetry in the theater," (*Off Broadway*, p. 52 ff.) he makes it clear that he equates poetry with idea, theme—the best word, perhaps, vision:

> It is incumbent on the dramatist
> to be a poet, and incumbent on the poet
> to be a prophet, dreamer, and interpreter of
> the racial dream.

Anderson's concept of the nature of poetry is, in brief, Victorian. He writes, for the most part, a rather loose and innocuous blank verse which on many occasions rises to the emotional demands he places upon it and only seldom intrudes upon the conscious reader as a distraction.

He has, of course, been criticized, both favorably and unfavorably, for his verse. It has been pointed out, for instance, that his obvious imitation of Shakespeare is an annoying limitation, and there is justice in this criticism. Blank verse does sound strange coming from the characters who inhabit the lower depths of *Winterset*. Further, modern poetry, under the New Criticism, has become so specialized an art that we find it difficult to accept it in so public a place as the popular theater—unless it comes as an anachronistic *tour de force* from a Christopher Fry, or bearing the authority of a Great Poet like T. S. Eliot. In other words, we can accept a poet turned playwright, but not a playwright who wishes to elevate his dialogue with conventional meters.

If Anderson failed as a poetic dramatist, however, he did so because his theory of dramatic poetry grew out of his major strength as a playwright, for Anderson was a traditional writer in an age of change, a conservative thinker in an era of political and social utopianism. He wrote plays that dealt with what he believed were the permanent, the universal themes. His theory of tragedy is the classic one of European culture, and he employed a language that he thought was appropriate to it.

Comedy of Manners 1927-1939

by WELLER EMBLER

In his book *Youth and Life* (1913), Randolph Bourne, early apologist for the younger generation, offered the very acceptable idea that to be young—"To keep one's reactions warm and true"—was to be saved. Some happy turn of the cultural wheel in America in 1913 or thereabouts rewarded the younger generation with confidence and a refreshing breeziness with which to go about the pleasant business of shocking one's elders, especially those who wagged stern and ancient forefingers about the value of respectability. But as so often happens, the young of one generation become the middle-aged of the next; and by 1935 the best seller among the books was not at all enthusiastic about being twenty-one but insisted, rather, that *Life Begins at Forty*. Nevertheless, the years between World War I and World War II were memorable for many good reasons, not the least of which was the renascence in American literature sponsored and guided by the young writers.

There was, to be sure, preciosity, posturing, snobbishness, sophomoric melancholy, and sentimentality; but mainly there was hope, hope that tomorrow will be more fun than today. Youth took over the responsibility for living and loving because there was so much to love and to live for and because the older generation had deliberately, it seemed, neglected its duty toward the arts of life and love. If there was dancing, it was by no means on the edge of the grave; war or no war, grim as were the battle-fields of France, there was hope, hope for a happier future, in which indeed there would be no wars. Man was not made for gloom, and H. L. Mencken created the perfect scapegoat, the stereotype of a dour, beauty-hating, hypocritical "puritan." Man, or at least youth, was born to be gay, to have many fetes, to be witty, to be poets, to be rich and fanciful. There was, too, in the wide various world of the twentieth century always the possibility of romance, the kind of incredibly beautiful romance that F. Scott Fitzgerald's characters were searching for, and when they did not find it despaired.

But the price exacted of youthful hope is heavy indeed. The more one expects and the less he succeeds in achieving, the more the disenchantment, unless through just this disillusion one succeeds in becoming a philosopher. The contour of literary history in America in the first half of the twentieth century is a dramatic curve of this kind—a rising action of accomplishment in the name of youth and hope, a falling denouement of disillusion and futility, and a curtain for the end of an era.[1]

Comedy in the American theatre flourished during the years between 1914 and 1939. There were many expert writers for the comic theatre, most of them young men and women.[2] It is of the three who came perhaps closest to the creation of traditional high comedy that we shall speak in this chapter—Philip Barry, Robert Emmet Sherwood, and S. N. Behrman. And of the three, it may as well be said at the outset, only S. N. Behrman is likely to remain as a first-rate writer of genuine high comedy in the history of American dramatic literature.

You and I (1923) was Philip Barry's first successful play; his last play, *Second Threshold,* was produced in 1951 two years after his death. Barry devoted more than twenty-five years to telling the story of high society in America, an entertaining story, but as it seems to us today not as important and not as mature as at the time it was considered to be.

Wealthy, talented, a graduate of Yale in the class of 1919 and then until 1922 a student in George Pierce Baker's 47 Workshop at Harvard, during the dozen years from *Paris Bound* in 1927 to *Philadelphia Story* in 1939, Philip Barry was (as agreed upon by both critics and public) Broadway's foremost writer of comedy of manners. His plays were in the tradition of high comedy, his class the leisure class, his scenes Park Avenue, the Riviera, the estates of the Philadelphia *beau monde,* the settings elegant and fashionable, the manners of his characters sophisticated, gay, gallant, witty, the mood lightly despairing, the philosophy the right to be oneself and to do as one pleases with one's life and money.

Two major themes of high comedy, from Moliere to S. N. Behrman, are the war of the sexes and the war of the generations. Barry devotes himself generously to both.

In the conflict between the sexes, Barry has this to offer: possessiveness in woman is her "lowest instinct" and needs to be dealt with accordingly. The male should be allowed to wander more or less as he feels he must and as he can afford. Infidelity, impromptu and meaningless, should not be grounds for severing the marriage tie. This is a main theme in both *Paris Bound* and *Philadelphia Story*.[3] In *Paris Bound* (1927), the play that established Barry firmly on Broadway, Jim is twenty-six and Mary is twenty-two when the play opens in a fashionable house in the country. They have just been married and are lyrically happy. Gifted with all they need to make a successful marriage—"youth, health, love, money, and an occupation," and armed with these securities, they sally forth to meet the world of adult responsibilities. Five years elapse between the first and second acts and all is still well until Jim, during various business trips to Europe, enters upon extra-marital relations with a former sweetheart somewhere in the Riviera. Mary learns of this defection through friends. Twenty-seven years old now and the mother of two children, she has altered her earlier convictions about the advisability of latitudinarianism in marriage and decides to divorce Jim. In the meantime, however, she has herself become strongly attached to an indigent young composer in whom she has taken a charitable and as it turns out amorous interest. Realizing that she is capable of such feelings toward a man other than her husband, and scolded by her father-in-law for her obstinacy and prudishness, Mary concludes that casual adultery is nothing like so serious a business as divorce. When Jim returns from his latest business trip, she says nothing to him about his straying, and he in turn, suspecting that there may have been something between Mary and the composer friend, says nothing, and they resume the mutually respectful and happy marital relations they have always enjoyed.

Several major elements of Barry's comedy of manners are gathered together in *Paris Bound*. There is the emphasis on youth, the importance of freedom from Victorian restraints, well-bred charm in the main characters, an inclination toward the bohemian, a neatly constructed plot, and the famous Barry dialogue that rolls so trip-

pingly off the tongues of good actors. Barry did not in *Paris Bound*
visit his scorn upon later favorite enemies: the parvenue American
business man (*Philadelphia Story*, 1939); the "puritan" devotion
to the ethic of work (*The Animal Kingdom*, 1932); and the empty
existence of the man in the gray-striped trousers, the main burden
of *Holiday*, 1928.[4]

Though Barry is better known for his polite comedies, *Hotel
Universe* (1930) and *Here Come the Clowns* (1938) are important plays, not least because they describe that path to wisdom
known as disillusion. Of hope there had been aplenty in the earlier
plays, of hope there is not much in these. But there is a tenderness
in *Hotel Universe* and a humanity in *Here Come the Clowns* not
found in the self-assured drawing-rooms of the smart-set comedies.

Neither of these two plays has been much admired by the
critics. Though Joseph Wood Krutch often had praise for Barry as
a playwright, he refers to *Hotel Universe* as "pretentious pseudo-
philosophy" and to *Here Come the Clowns* as the "speculations of
an amateur theologian." From the point of view of philosophy and
theology, Krutch may be close to the mark; but the social message is
clear enough. One might understand the play to say this, that it is
at home, the home where one *lives*, that we find our happiness or
not at all.

In a letter to his daughter in the fall of 1937, F. Scott Fitzgerald wrote, "I have seen the whole racket, and if there is any
more disastrous road than that from Park Avenue to the Rue de la
Paix and back again, I don't know it. . . . They are homeless people,
ashamed of being American, unable to master the culture of another
country." In *Hotel Universe,* the group assembled on the terrace of an
elegant house in the south of France is made up of expatriates, rich,
witty, cosmopolitan. But they are older now than they were in
Paris Bound and in *Holiday*. They are the lost generation, and
during the evening there is talk of suicide and attempted suicide,
talk about the meaninglessness of life, and about the search for
identity. With these sensitive and idle rich, something has come to an
end; but Barry suggests that there may still be somewhere for them
a new dawn. The war of the sexes enjoys an armistice here,
so too the war of the generations. Instead, the defeated have a charm
that comes of the author's compassion. Though Barry has in *Hotel
Universe* and in *Here Come the Clowns* done the one thing a
writer of high comedy ought not to have done, lose his detachment

and enter into the sufferings of his characters, there is a warmth in these plays that is not found elsewhere in his work.

Philip Barry and Robert Emmet Sherwood were born in the same year, 1896, Barry in Rochester, Sherwood in New Rochelle, New York. Barry went to Yale, Sherwood to Harvard. Both served in World War I, Sherwood with the Royal Highlanders of Canada, Barry in the State Department in Washington and at the American Embassy in London. While Barry was studying with Baker in the 47 Workshop at Harvard, Sherwood was movie and drama critic first for *Vanity Fair* and then for *Life* and the New York *Herald*. Sherwood's first popular success was in 1927, *The Road to Rome*, Barry's first, *Paris Bound* in the same year. Both were idealists, very much on the side of youth and life, determined to keep their reactions "warm and true." Both had contempt for intolerance, big business, and the money-making complacency of their elders. In the 30's both turned to the description of disenchanment and the search for new ideals. Both were capable of sentimentality; both were writers of fluent dialogue; both were virtuosos of stagecraft; both were admired by critics; and both were fortunate in having actors of rare quality and skill in the production of their plays on Broadway. Philip Barry died in 1949 at the age of fifty-three. Robert E. Sherwood six years later at the age of fifty-nine.

Attentively aware of the political state of the world, Sherwood introduced a high seriousness into his plays, a seriousness relieved now and again by farce, reinforced now and again by sentimentality and melodrama, always supported by a studied showmanship.

The Road to Rome (1927) is a play with a war in the background, but the essential conflict is between the hero, Carthaginian Hannibal, and the heroine, Amytis, wife of the Roman dictator Fabius Maximus. It is not so much that Amytis wishes to save Rome that she goes to Hannibal's camp as that she wishes to learn the secret of Hannibal's power and then destroy it—and destroy it she does. The war on the stage is the war of the sexes, with the woman, as in most Sherwood plays, victorious.

Reunion in Vienna (1931) confirmed Sherwood's place on Broadway as a writer of continental comedies, as "continental" says Krutch, "as though he had been born in Budapest." But there is less to *Reunion in Vienna* than meets the eye. It has undeniable charm, at times, and it attacks with expert showmanship and, in 1931, brilliant actors (Lynn Fontanne and Alfred Lunt), the know-it-all complacency of the new psychology and the new middle-class psychiatrist. But *Reunion in Vienna* is not Ferenc Molnar or Arthur Schnitzler. The hero, exiled Archduke Rudolf, is more like a Restoration rakehell in London of 1670 than Schnitzler's graceful and cynical Anatol of aristocratic Vienna. The tumbling is rather more like a Broadway bedroom farce brought up-to-date for the sophisticated American audience of 1931 than the dextrous and subtle intriguing in the plots of Ferenc Molnar. But it was a good show, risque, vivacious, hardhitting, with the heroine always quite in command of the domestic and amorous situations.

The conflict of cultural ideals in the play is presented with admirable simplicity. Dr. Anton Krug, the psychiatrist, is a nice chap but rather too over-confident of his knowledge of human behavior. As a result, he is cuckolded in his own bed, having left his wife and her former lover alone in his house for the night on the theory that the confrontation between them, after the years of separation and now that they are older, will cure each of any desire the one may have for the other. As might be expected, it turns out that Dr. Krug is mistaken.

Idiot's Delight (1936) is an anti-militarist play with a vigorous anti-Fascist postscript in the printed version. The scene is a cocktail lounge in the Hotel Gabriele in the Italian Alps. Harry Van has arrived with his six blonde chorus girls. Harry is "a thoughtful, lonely American vaudevillian promoter," crooner, hoofer, and barker. He and his girls have been playing "the Balkan circuit" with a routine honky-tonk show. At one point during the action of the play, Harry and his troupe put on a song and dance number for the guests of the Hotel, an ingenious theatrical device, since the dancing and singing are being played against a background of anxiety, rumors of international war, rifle shots of execution, and the proximity of Italian fascist soldiers.

Among the guests is a munitions tycoon and his mistress, Irene, who says she is a Russian princess, but who turns out to be a show girl with whom Harry Van was once in love and with whom he had once slept in a hotel room in Omaha, Nebraska. At the end of the play, the munitions magnate abandons Irene because of her display of pacifistic ideas, and Harry sends his girls off to safety, while he and Irene remain at the Hotel awaiting the bombing raid that is to be almost certain death for them. Harry is at the piano and Irene stands near him as several loud explosions are heard off stage. She says, "Harry, do you realize that the whole world has gone to war? *The whole world!*" While the sounds of the raid continue, Harry plays "Onward, Christian Soldiers" in a "furious jazz time" and then in a "slow, solemn tempo" as he and Irene sing the hymn together and the curtain falls.

This is theatre in the American tradition of comedy-melodrama. The stagecraft is facile, the dramatic situations expertly designed to entertain while at the same time the grim theme of war, like the sound of aircraft in the background, comes steadily and irremediably closer. The comic hero moves bravely through the scenes, a sentimental master of ceremonies who already knows the outcome of the evening's entertainment. *Idiot's Delight* may well be Sherwood's best play, but as with *The Petrified Forest* there is a pervading mood of futility in it, that same confession of defeat to be found in so many of the young writers of the 20's as they moved along in the anxious frightened decade of the 30's.[5]

After plays like *Idiot's Delight* and *The Petrified Forest*, "the wonder is," as Eleanor Flexner says in her *American Playwrights: 1918-1938*, "that Mr. Sherwood ever pulled himself together to crack another joke." But like many of his expatriate contemporaries, Sherwood re-discovered America in the late 30's, and this was a vitalizing experience. Unwilling to be victimized by the intellectual's mood of despair, he sought and found new values in the American scene, and he richly deserved the Pulitzer Prize for *Abe Lincoln in Illinois* in 1938. It is not surprising that he should have devoted himself during the war years to working with President Roosevelt for those freedoms they both believed in, freedom from want and freedom from fear, for with these freedoms the world just *might* be a decent place to live in.

Samuel Nathaniel Behrman, born in Worcester, Massachusetts, in 1893, graduated from Harvard in 1916, studied with George Pierce Baker in the 47 Workshop at Harvard, worked toward an M.A. degree at Columbia University where he took courses with Brander Matthews and John Erskine, and enjoyed his first Broadway success in 1927 with the Theatre Guild's production of his play *The Second Man*.

Barry, Sherwood, and Behrman had similar educational and social backgrounds. They attended famous eastern universities, all were young men in the 20's, all were devoted to literature and the cultivated life of their time, all prized the urbanity and sophistication of cosmopolitanism. Most significant, perhaps, was their early attachment to the cultural ideals of the genteel tradition in Boston and New York. It is not surprising that their early aspirations were toward high comedy, as high comedy is the form the genteel tradition takes when it becomes dramatic.

The genteel tradition depends on wealth and social homogeneity, on cultivated and expensive tastes, on good form as a style of human behavior, often represented in ceremony, elegant and complicated. "The aim of its social philosophy is happiness. and though as a way of life the tradition seeks to avoid the unpleasant, if necessary by overlooking it, nevertheless, the genteel tradition trusts in the good things of life, believes in being civilized, and is devoted, in a naive sort of way, to the idea of good will toward men."[7] When the tradition is represented in the theatre, the dramatic structure and point of view usually follow the celebrated analysis of the comic spirit made by George Meredith in his *Essay on Comedy* written in the late nineteenth century when the tradition was articulated brilliantly, for example, in the novels and stories of Henry James.

Of the three writers of comedy we are discussing in this chapter, S. N. Behrman is the most at home in the genteel tradition and the most consistent philosopher of the comic spirit as a way of life. All three tried to be patient and understanding students of human folly after the manner of Meredith's *Essay,* but only Behrman succeeded in holding to his detachment and maintaining the life style of the comic spirit in the face of the vast social changes that have taken place since 1927. This is not to say that he has ignored change or escaped from it; on the contrary he has kept a sharp analytical eye on the modern world.

Behrman has seldom depended upon theatrical devices, and his dialogue is literary with emphasis on the epigrammatic rather than on the wisecrack or quick retort. His wit, wisdom, and dramatic situations grow out of the characters he has chosen to write about. The people who inhabit his drawing-rooms are literate and civilized people of the twentieth century. His society is that "of cultivated men and women . . . wherein ideas are current, and perceptions quick," the kind of society, as Meredith says, essential to the writer of high comedy. The situations in which the extremists among these people find themselves, in which indeed they have put themselves because they are extreme in their behavior, are the standard ones of high comedy—the war of the generations, the war of the sexes, fanaticism versus the middle way of compromise and common sense, the conflict between boorish *arrivistes* and the traditions of the cultivated, the unmasking of self-delusion, the value of tolerance and good-nature over stubbornness and hardness of heart, the cosmopolitan versus the parochial point of view.

Behrman's immediate milieu is that of wealth, good taste, and modishness, but the larger *mise-en-scene* of his plays is the state of the world by which his characters are surrounded and about which they are very articulate. Through the subtle insights of the playwright as detached observer, his plays are marked by extraordinary anticipation of social change. In *Meteor* (1929), Behrman may be said to have made telling note of the inevitability of the financial collapse of the American economy in the 30's; in *Brief Moment* (1931), he watches the downward path of the idle rich to social emptiness; in *Biography* (1932), he satirizes the childishness and comic self-delusion of the American male as big-business man and politician;[8] in *Rain from Heaven* (1934), he observes the fascist origins of World War II; in *End of Summer* (1936), he is already aware of the coming existentialist search for identity and the coming need for the courage to be-as-oneself; and in *No Time for Comedy* (1939), he foretells the end of the comic spirit as a way of life in the modern world.

Rain from Heaven is, perhaps, Behrman's best play, certainly the portraits of the people assembled for the occasion in the drawing-room of Lady Wyngate's country house outside London in 1934 are among his most sensitive delineations. Writing in *Vanity Fair* in March, 1935, George Jean Nathan said of *Rain From Heaven,* "It is a testimonial to [Behrman's] fine honesty, very considerable skill in drawing character in short, sharp strokes, high gift for dialogue, and steadfast avoidance of every trace and smell of facile theatrical sham."

The problems of the world of 1934 are brought into sharp dramatic focus in the conflicts that dominate the stage in *Rain from Heaven.* The people at Lady Wyngate's house represent international high society caught up in the fierce antagonisms and prejudices of their time, some capable of penetrating insights into their predicament. One of the memorable moments of the theatre of high comedy comes at the end of the second act. Lady Wyngate, wealthy but inclined to the new socialism, a woman of very considerable personal distinction, has been quite stupidly and wrongly accused, by her attractive young American suitor, of having an affair with one of her guests, the German refugee scholar Hugo Willens. In a fit of anger, the young man (hero of an Antarctic expedition) shouts at

Willens, "You God damned Jew!" In the awful silence that follows,
Lady Wyngate gently takes the hand of the exiled Willens and, as
they leave the room together, says, "Remember, please, Mr. Willens
is not only my lover; he is also my guest."

It is not difficult to imagine what would have happened to this
scene in the hands of a less accomplished writer. As it stands, it
is witness to Behrman's mastery of the form we know as "high comedy."

Melodrama, farce, vaudeville, song and dance have been abundant in the history of the American theatre. These are the forms
indigenous to the American way of life, authentic expressions of
a culture and genuine contributions to the history of theatre. High
comedy, or comedy of manners, is not native to American culture
and did not appear until the twentieth century when a few young
playwrights chose this way of talking about human relations and
turned for inspiration to old-world traditions of high comedy. Comedy of manners had its brief moment at a time when theatre-goers
wished to think of themselves as sophisticated in the continental
manner; but since 1939 there have been very few high comedies of
distinction in the American theatre.[9] The theatre returned, because
it had to, to its own traditions with which to express the evils and
confusions besetting the modern world, to melodrama, to farce-
comedy, to the topical review, and to the sentiment, humor, song
and dance of the musicals.

Today, the nearest thing we have to polite comedy is the musical. Being native to American culture, it expresses the humor,
good-nature, charm, and high spirits not wholly lacking in American
life even in a time of troubles, and does so better than continental
comedy of manners ever could. In any case, at the moment, as the
title of one of S. N. Behrman's plays says, this is no time for
high comedy. The unbane banter of idle cosmopolitans is not only
beside the point, it is, in its reflection of the comic spirit of tolerant
detachment, futile and ineffectual. Still, it seems a pity that the
silent laughter of literate observers should have to give way completely before the "black" comedy of the theatres of cruelty and
the absurd.

FOOTNOTES

1. There was, to be sure, the new hope that sprang from the social ideals
of the 30s, but that was the beginning of something else, having, too, its
brief moment in the sun.

2. For example, George S. Kaufman, Edna Ferber, Ring Lardner, George Kelly, Sidney Howard, Marc Connelly, Moss Hart, Rachel Crothers, Clare Boothe.

3. The theme of female possessiveness is also major in *Holiday* (1928) and *The Animal Kingdom* (1932). In these plays it is presented in terms of the domineering wife, or wife-to-be, who tries to make her husband over into the kind of man she thinks he ought to be.

4. In *Holiday*, Johnny Case gives up the beautiful and possessive twenty-eight-year-old Julia Seton and her millions and an opportunity (a requirement in this instance) to join her father's law firm because he does not want to "settle down," as he must if he is to marry Julia, to the ritual of money-making. He prefers holidays instead.

5. In *The Petrified Forest* (1935), Alan Squire is "looking for something to believe in—something that's worth living for—and dying for." A sensitive intellectual, Squire is surrounded by crudeness and violence. His day is over, and indeed it is, as the anarchic guns of the gangster killer shoot him down. "Whirl is King, having driven out Zeus" would have served as well as a motto for *The Petrified Forest* as it did for Walter Lippmann's book, well-known at the time, *A Preface to Morals* (1929).

6. An interesting study could be made of the effect of the dramatic theories of George Pierce Baker and Brander Matthews on the theatre of the 20s and 30s. Both teachers wrote distinguished textbooks on playwriting, Baker *Dramatic Technique* (1919) and Matthews *The Principles of Playmaking* (1919), and both had pupils who were to become successful playwrights. There may be something in the logic of their dramatic principles that reflects the cultural milieu of the time, a logic which the sensitive young writer could see and accept.

7. For a somewhat more extended analysis of the genteel tradition, see Weller Embler, *Metaphor and Meaning*, DeLand, Florida, 1966, pgs. 15ff.

8. As observed earlier in this chapter, a prevailing element in comedy is the war of the sexes; but for comedy to be truly high, there must be equality between the sexes, and on the surface this is the case in the plays of Barry, Sherwood, and Behrman. A little study, however, will reveal that this is not always the case, and in Behrman particularly, the woman is invariably presented as superior in intelligence to the male. In *Biography* the heroine, Marion Froude, international portrait painter, is astonishingly skillful in her handling of the male—the American male, that is, for her Viennese are models of maturity, tolerance, and cultivation. Indeed, from one point of view she is an opportunist, rather heartless, capricious, contriving, and not a little malicious. Her techniques are not always subtle, at least to the audience, though they may be to the other characters involved in the dramatic situations. She is skilful at humiliation and carries off the manner of superiority with distinction. Her consistent attitude is that the man is a grown-up child who needs to be punished or stroked as the case may be. For one who had the good fortune to see the accomplished actress Ina Claire in the role of Marion Froude in 1932, it is easy to recall just how carefully Behrman delineated his main character. In doing this, however, he neglected the men and they are types of childishness rather than fully-characterized men sometimes behaving like children, and in any case by no means Marion's equal in intelligence.

9. It is not entirely facetious to suggest that as a textbook for playwrights, *Games People Play* by Eric Berne (New York, 1964) would serve better today than anything written by George Pierce Baker or Brander Matthews. When we wish to analyze our social behavior with scientific detachment (the

comic spirit in the social sciences), we listen quite seriously to Dr. Berne who talks about human behavior and human relations in terms of programing, data processing, sorting and classifying—high comedy in the computer laboratory. The marital psychotherapy group becomes the modern substitute for comedy of manners in a system known as transactional psychology.

Through a Glass Menagerie Darkly: the World of Tennessee Williams

by SY KAHN

I am convinced that Williams is the most important playwright writing in America today, and that when a final assessment is made of American dramatic literature of the 20th Century, he and Eugene O'Neill will stand as our most powerful playwrights. I confess, I once thought it would be Arthur Miller, but Williams has the staying power—or is it the obsession—the fertility, the inventiveness to assure him first rank as a writer. Miller has written great plays; so have others. But I am talking here of the range and total production of a writer's work, and I see no other playwright in America as yet who can seriously challenge Williams and O'Neill. I wish to defend Williams' work, partly because, as with many outstanding writers, he has been the target of frequent attack and denigration by the world at large, and by many professional critics. He has been accused of enough sins and outrages to occupy all the circles of Dante's Hell, but especially of preoccupation with sex, vulgarity, violence, obscenity and grotesque distortions of the human psyche. People who have never seen a Williams play object to him and have their clichéd preconceptions which, of course, is evidence

71

of his considerable impact on our society. For many he is the *bête noir* of contemporary literature and a moral deformity. Since I feel that the charges against him are half-truths at best, and usually based upon an essentially naive and irrelevant attitude toward literature and its function, I wish to defend him, and especially against all those whose concept of literature is that it be morally edifying rather than a source of insight into the human condition. And lastly I wish to defend him because I believe the true function of the critic is to serve the artist and his work by making it more accessible to an audience, not to use it or him to demonstrate the critic's superior mind or to discharge his hostility and ire. For me, the artist is one of the most valuable members of a society, the tongue and sometimes the conscience of the race. The critic *serves* the art, if he means to do it a service. As the Finnish composer Sibelius once said, in suffering adverse criticism in his own time, "Who ever built a statue to a critic?"

In commenting upon Williams, I do want to make clear that I am writing about his world as rendered by his work as a writer. What I do want to correct is an over simplification of his work and an easy, misinformed moralistic judgment of his plays. Something of the pervasive general attitude toward the man and his work is revealed, I think, by a story recently told to me. It seems that a panhandler approached a well-dressed lady and asked her for a dime. The lady backed away a step, looked the ragged man up and down, and imperiously said, "Waste not, want not: William Shakespeare." After a moment the panhandler also took a step backwards, looked the lady up and down, and retorted, "Lady, go to Hell: Tennessee Williams." Now I am not prepared to say that Williams is the greatest writer since Shakespeare, as John O'Hara flamboyantly said of Ernest Hemingway some years ago, but a playwright of major importance he certainly is, and, I contend, will be in our literary history.

A Mississippian by birth, a world wanderer by choice, Thomas Lanier Williams is fifty-two years old.[1] He briefly attended the University of Missouri, later Washington University in St. Louis, and received his B.A. degree from the University of Iowa when he was twenty-four years old. The offspring of a shoe salesman and of the daughter of an Episcopalian minister, he has never married. Though his literary reputation rests mainly upon his work as a

---

1. This essay was written in 1965.

playwright, he has also published poems, short stories and one novel, *The Roman Spring of Mrs. Stone*. As is the case with most writers, Williams did not burst upon the literary scene fully armed with the skills of a playwright. He served a long apprenticeship and wrote scores of scenarios and had a number of productions in small community and independent theaters. However, from the outset his plays aroused an excited response and gave people the sense that a fresh, vital talent was in their presence. It was clear from the beginning that his work was particularly strong in dialogue, exactly where a playwright must be no less than good if he hopes to succeed. Before he attained spectacular success, he received modest grants from the Group Theater and the Rockefeller Foundation, but scarcely enough to keep him from necessarily working as a waiter in New Orleans, later in Greenwich Village, for seventeen dollars a week.

In 1940, when he was twenty-six, his play *Battle of Angels* opened in Boston, his first major production. Simply put, Williams conceived the play as the tragedy of a wandering poet who incurs his own punishment by bringing to a love-starved Southern woman both her salvation and destruction. The opening night was a fiasco. First shocked into hostile silence, the audience hissed and booed until the actors' words were drowned out. Williams recalled, "I never heard of an audience getting so infuriated. The reactions made Miriam [Hopkins] so mad she began to scream her lines above the hissing. Then they stamped their feet, and after a while most of them got up and left, banging their seats behind them." Some people shook their fists at the stage. Then the smoke pots got out of hand and billows filled the stage and the house. The already outraged audience, breathing smoke, spluttered out of the theater, and the next day the critics continued to splutter in the reviews. Further, the play came under attack from both the Watch and Ward Society and the Boston City Council. Thus a quarter of a century ago Williams learned a hard lesson: for an American audience, and particularly a Boston audience, the mixture of sex and religion was an incendiary, explosive combination. The incident of the runaway smudge pots now seems a beautifully appropriate symbol. Despite this disaster, Williams has continued to work the themes into various dramatic configurations, and the fires have continued to burn and the acid smoke billow. At twenty-six Williams seemed not to be totally aware of how sensitive an area he had probed with this play. Our history reveals the sharpest division between matters sexual and matters theological, and in marrying the themes of sex and religion, what he attempted to join, most Americans had always attempted to put asunder. To Williams, the play was an attempt to render human longings and the sometimes conflicting desire of the flesh and spirit. But as he says, ". . . I never dreamed that such struggles could strike many people as filthy and seem to them unfit for articulation." For him, the play was "clean" and even "idealistic," and the experience of writing it was like "taking a bath in snow."

Despite Williams' defeat with *Battle of Angels* in the battle of Boston, the next quarter of a century was to bring him many successes, both literary and financial. Since that smoky opening he has had fourteen full-length plays produced in major productions, most of them opening in New York City, and countless productions of his work in theaters all over the country and the world, as well as translations of many of his plays into films. Let me briefly list the kind of recognition he has received. In 1944 The American Academy of Arts and Letters awarded him $1000. In 1945 *The Glass Menagerie* won the New York Critics' Circle Award and the fourth annual award of the *Catholic Monthly* as well as the Sidney Howard Memorial Award given by the Playwright's Company; in 1947 *Streetcar Named Desire* won a second New York Critics' Circle Award and a Pulitzer Prize; in 1952 he was elected to the exclusive National Institute of Arts and Letters; in 1955 *Cat on a Hot Tin Roof* won a third New York Critics' Circle Award and a second Pulitzer Prize. Thus at forty-one Tennessee Williams had won five major awards and become the best known American dramatist of the decade. This record speaks to his success as a playwright in spite of his detractors.

A number of reasons account for Williams' success, aside from his fine ear for dialogue, his sharp eye for the particularities of character, and his creative, plastic use of stage settings and mood. There are several basic assumptions from which his plays are constructed which touch at the center of American life. I want to discuss these, but first make the observation that most writers do not have a great stock and range of ideas. Examine the total work of a writer and frequently one will discover a small cluster of essential ideas and experiences which motivate and energize his total production. These central ideas and experiences are often of a traumatic nature, and the writer works numerous variations from this same basic material, obsessively replaying, as it were, compulsively acting out the original, interior drama. The artist is able, through his craft and imagination, to shape the plots, characters and symbols that give form to his central tensions. Should these dilemmas be the same as those shared by many others, and should they be of a more or less equally secret, repressed, interior nature, the shock of recognition for the audience, and the discovery that one is not as alienated as one supposed, help guarantee the success of the work.

For example, Arthur Miller's *Death of a Salesman* succeeds magnificently because Willie Loman's dreams, defeat and death make manifest the unvoiced fears of so many who, like Willy, suspect they have the wrong dream, and suspect too that the American gospel of material success and of being well-liked is a swindle. Thus the unfolding of Willy's disillusion and defeat dramatizes the nagging, latent nightmare that haunts many of the audience. The play provides an image of the inevitable end of the road that many have chosen, and the dreadful recognition that perhaps they have used their lives for shoddy and meaningless purposes. Similarly, Williams' traumas and insights, and the dramas shaped from them, give us viable, strong images of our deep anxieties, and that is why, for example, his neurotic, delicate, frangible Southern women have had wide identification and appeal. They are our anxieties fleshed. The plays hit hard and deep. Consequently we may not always like them, but we do not easily forget them, any more than we can forget ourselves, because they are, in a curious way, our most intimate selves.

Since few Americans have grown up in our country without feeling the painful pressures that our Puritan and Victorian heritage have exerted on them, Williams' tormented, deeply ambivalent women and his emotionally, and sometimes literally, castrated men speak vitally to our dilemmas. The pressures I am talking about are those that repress sex, that impel us toward social status and wealth, that make us suspect that the flesh is the basic cause of evil behavior, that compel us to judge ourselves and each other, and to cure our moral infirmities. All this demands a constant and painful psychic surgery. I am suggesting that the American fascination with human psychology, with psychiatry, with sociology, with American Studies, which often involves an analysis of American character, are impelled by the obsession to explore and to bring to light the sources of the forces we so uncomfortably live with, and by recognizing them, resolve them. Except, except, except . . . our intellectuality, our shrewder and shrewder and more refined and sophisticated methods of analysis seldom solve and resolve the problems, and the final fact is that reason, in which we characteristically put so much faith, continues to analyze endlessly, even insanely, while we continue to be driven and fated by the guilts, the needs, the aspirations and hungers that have emotionally and psychically shaped us. How well those ancient and wily Greeks, along with their thrust toward reason and logic, understood the dilemma. Every reading of Plato and Aristotle should be balanced by Aeschylus and Euripides to learn what is really going on! To change even a little, to alter one contour of our emotional profile, to resolve one dilemma requires revelation more than reason, requires desire not didacticism, demands faith not analysis—and there lies a mystery that defies our powers of reason and our best reasoners. Thus Williams' outrageous plays and seemingly bizarre characters speak eloquently to our intimate, secret, personal dilemmas, and, at their best moments, speak also to the more universal human condition.

Discerning people always discover that the poet knows our ailments and our problems, and that ultimately the canvas, the contoured clay, the luminous play, the piercing musical passage, the poem that falls on the heart like a stone—or like a flower—tells us the real story, that our mystery is best revealed by the mystery, and the necessary craft to shape it, of the poet's statement. It is the artist's power of prophecy, his power to intuitively divine the truth, and perhaps that which is divine itself, his power of incantation, his power to take the bare stage and raise spectres and visions, and by means of them images of truth and reality, his power to reveal truth by illusion, that makes art, and particularly the drama, the cathartic, cleansing, illuminating agent it can be. And because the artist is something of an alchemist, a sorcerer whose fictions and metaphors are the calculated strategies and lies by which the truth may be revealed, so he often dramatizes himself in his work as an eccentric or unusually gifted figure: the wandering traveller-poet, the clown, the hobo, the singer, the witch, the prophet, the afflicted, the strange healer.

In his plays Williams' most frequent mask is the vulnerable poet-wanderer, who sees the center of our confusions and dilemmas from his position of a fringe member of the society. Because the artist knows he possesses and expresses dangerous truths, he knows he is exceptionally vulnerable. Among hunters, it is the bird that sings and reveals his position that is slain. Because man cannot stand too much truth and only a little reality, and tends to destroy those that threaten him with truth, the writer often prefigures his own death in the destruction of his dramatic masks, the symbols of himself. And something primitive, barbaric is satisfied by witnessing in the dark theater the death of the truth-bearer. We are washed clean in his blood. Like the crippled god Vulcan, the master artificer, the most artistically gifted of the old gods, the artist's persona is often cast as some sort of cripple or as a person whose truth is misapprehended, as if his talent and insight demand a punishing disability. So Teiresias, who sees all, and who was both man and woman, is blind; so Cassandra, who could foretell the truth, was cursed so that she would never be believed by her audience, and ultimately is murdered by them, so the clown, who, with his antics makes the crowd laugh at his contortions, rarely receives the recognition of his great gift and craft; so Williams' fragile heroes and heroines break up like glass as they are thrown against the iron walls of ordinary reality. To the hard eye of the world they are the ridiculous and ridiculed outcasts, kept at a safe distance, starved to submission and to death. Socrates drank the hemlock and Christ was nailed to the wood because they insisted on being real, and we know in our heart of hearts that to be real is to risk injury and death, not to mention ridicule and ostracism, which are stations along the way. In a poem called "The Beanstalk Country" Williams gives us an image of the person who sees into or above the ordinary reality, and the fate of the seer with the searing vision.

> You know how the mad come into a room,
> Too boldly,
> Their eyes exploding on the air like roses,
> their entrances from space we never entered.
> They're always attended by someone small and friendly
> who goes between their awful world and ours
> as though explaining but really only smiling,
> a snowy gull that dips above a wreck.
>
> They see not us, nor any Sunday caller
> among the geraniums and wicker chairs,
> for they are the Jacks who climb the beanstalk country,
> a place of hammers and tremendous beams,
> compared to which the glassed solarium
> in which we rise to greet them has no light.

The news we bring them, common, reassuring,
drenched with the cheerful idiocy of noon,
cannot compete with what they have to tell of what they saw
through cracks in the ogre's oven.

And we draw back. The snowy someone says,
Don't mind their talk, they are disturbed today!

What are the themes obsessive in Williams' work, the discoveries of this mad Jack in the beanstalk country, and why is that work considered dangerous and outrageous by many, and why does that work enchant us and insinuate itself into our hearts and minds? All these questions are answered, I think, if we now consider the central themes of Williams' work which structure his world.

The strongest of these is the theme of human sexuality. Most of Williams' major characters suffer the most excruciating ambivalencies because of their guilt about their sex drives and needs. His plays speak eloquently of the emotional tension and psychological disfigurement caused by the suppression of sexual forces. On the other hand, when a character has sexual freedom, he then becomes the target of all those who envy that freedom, who consider it a threat to their own lives, an indictment of their own fears and inhibitions, as well as a cultural outrage. Such a character frequently ends up brutally punished and savagely tortured. He is purged from the community in order to preserve the puritanical-victorian codes of purity. Also, the victim's torment pays for the guilt of the sexual indiscretions of his tormentors, as well as, in a twisted, sadistic way, expresses their repressed sexuality. That is the fate of some of Williams' hero-victims.

The women are usually more subtly tortured. Torn between the demands of social and moral codes and carnal and emotional needs, they torment themselves. Put another way, if you like, but all too simply, the super-ego and id battle within the fallen angel. These women too may become victims of those in the society whose need is less, whose power of suppression is greater, whose sexual satisfactions have been sublimated. If the victim is weak, if her emotional resources have been exhausted or eroded, she can be driven insane, even killed. If she is strong, she can become rapacious, punishing, nervous but crafty as a cat on a hot tin roof. She can destroy a man to find a mate, or she can destroy him because he will not mate.

In Williams' world there is the male fear of entrapment by women, reminiscent of some D. H. Lawrence and Bernard Shaw male characters. Their male heroes, along with Williams', tend to be poet-wanderers, desperate to maintain their freedom and creative energies, needing women, but fearing their need to encapsulate the man. "All women," says Shannon, in *The Night of the Iguana,* symbolically tied up in a hammock, "love nothing better than getting, seeing a man in a tied-up situation." He rants that "they work at it all their lives, to get one man, or as many men as they can, in the tied-up situation." And Hannah Jelkes, from her cool, celibate heights, must agree that it is true for most women, though not for her. The men fear that their search, their creative trust will be sacrificed to the desperate need of the woman for permanence and a total relationship with the man, rather than only a sexual one. Williams' allegorical poem "Everyman" speaks precisely to the point:

> I went to the house of Everyman,
> I found his woman there.
> I asked her, Where is Everyman?
> She said, His home is air.

> I asked her, then, What is he like?
> She said, No woman knows.
> He moaned a little as he crept
> beneath my linen clothes.

> He lay upon me as a bird,
> She said with half disdain.
> Why, in the hurry of his wings
> he scarcely spoke my name!

> And when he left you, did you grieve?
> Oh, no, I scarcely knew . . .
> She rose, and to the window moved,
> indolent and huge . . .

> Then all at once her body broke
> in two parts, like a stone,
> and as the savage bird escaped,
> It's Everyman, she moaned.

To complete the variations on the theme: in Williams' world repression of sexual desire sometimes leads to perversion, sometimes to brutal substitutes for sexual excitement and satisfaction, sometimes to pathetic, bizarre, gentle oddities, as with the Australian salesman who takes Hannah Jelkes out in a sampan and derives his "satisfaction" by holding an article of her clothing. Sadness, pathos, brutality and savagery ring changes upon the theme; rape, immolation, crucifixion, human sacrifice, even cannibalism are its ultimate expression. Small wonder his dramas amaze, outrage, shock and intimidate as the dark side of our minds are turned up to the theater lights and, to many, indecently exposed. Man can stand only a little truth, a little reality. The need for human warmth, of which sex is a natural expression, and the fear and horror of the physical and the flesh are recurrent adversaries in human history. This central dilemma in many of Williams' plays is, of course, a basic and ancient conflict, as is the battle between the sexes which frequently has manifested the theme, but, as Williams understands and renders it, especially vicious in the American arena.

Williams is among those writers who have felt the deep tensions and problems associated with the battle of flesh and spirit. I think some critics have been wrong in judging Williams' dramas to be merely sex-ridden as a medieval monastery, as merely catering to a puerile, prurient, sensation-hungry audience. There is, I think, more wit than wisdom in Mary McCarthy's jibe that Williams' plays are rooted in *pay* dirt. I am much more in agreement with Esther Jackson in her book *The Broken World of Tennessee Williams* when she comments that he uses sex as a kind of glass through which he focuses his dark vision of man.

A second major theme in Williams' work and world is the horror of non-being. Often this is rendered as a sense of an underlying and pervasive terror, not quite explicable or explicit, but frequently felt by the characters who feel haunted, spooked by a sense of impending evil. Williams wrote in the preface to *The Rose Tattoo*, "As far as we know, as far as there exists any kind of empiric evidence, there is no way to beat the game of being against non-being, in which non-being is the predestined victor on realistic levels." Williams' lively awareness that death, and perhaps nothingness, are the ultimate destiny accounts for his sympathy for those characters who desperately cling to delicate, personal ideals, who assert their "beingness," even though their lives are brief candles doomed to darkness. Always there is something, he tells us in the mood and atmosphere of the play, that is brooding, terrible and malignant, that threatens and shadows the characters' lives—some secret cancer blooming silently in the dark blood, some lurking force hovering at the edge of the jungle setting. The sleepless man, aware of *nada*, familiar to the readers of Camus, Dostoyevsky, Kafka and Hemingway, is also a character in Williams' world. Along with the unsentimental awareness and response to the fact of death which informs these writers' works, it may be that Williams' awareness that man can perpetrate every sort of outrage upon his fellow man also accounts for the sense of a malign spirit in many of the plays. Speaking of man's mortality, he says, "This is God's or the devil's way of removing us to make room for our descendents. Do they work together, God and the devil? I sometimes suspect there is a sort of understanding between them, which we won't understand until Doomsday."

The malign atmosphere in his plays may be accounted for in still another way. Williams is a member of that remarkable group of 20th Century American writers who have come out of the South. He, like Carson McCullers, a close personal friend of his, like Truman Capote, Lillian Hellman and William Faulkner use the South as the proper setting for insanity and horror. (Standing, perhaps one should say *brooding,* behind them all is the dark ghost of Edgar Allen Poe.) To the extent that most of Williams' plays are set in the South, and his characters are Southern types, he may be called a regional writer, a local colorist. But to reduce his stature to these narrow confines would be as wrongheaded as to call William Faulkner merely a Southern writer. For both these major writers, it should be understood that the South is a microcosm, a little world in which the local drama suggests the macrocosm, the larger world. Those who would do less would probably also call *Moby Dick* the story of a big fish. For those writers of gothic imagination, for those who are spooked by a sense of evil and corruption, the South offers a convenient metaphor, because—and if you have lived in the South perhaps you have sensed it—the South, I insist, does give one the impression of a brooding spirit abroad in the land and a sense of decay. Perhaps it is the sultry heat, perhaps it is the ruined mansions, the weed-speared, abandoned shack, perhaps because the South lost the Civil War and a sullen rebellion still pervades the sun-baked town and town square where stands the inevitable stone confederate soldier, concretized image of lost causes and defeat; perhaps it is the presence of scarcely liberated Negroes, or the red-eyed viciousness of resentful white trash; perhaps it is the Spanish moss that hangs in the trees like the hair of witches, the miasma of the mangrove swamps, and the sweetness of night-blooming jasmine that perfumes the predatory night; perhaps it is political corruption, the sense of brutal power, perhaps the hard voices of fanatic fundamentalists, or the wailing ghosts of the lynched; perhaps it is the soft Southern speech, so often polite, honeyed, liquid—and so often deceptive. "Now suh—if yo' please, will y'all so kindly tell us the names of those po', misguided persons who suggested that *Catcher in the Rye* and *Streetcar Named Desire* was proper readin' for our white, Christian boys and girls?" While outside the interrogation room, on telephone poles is the sign: "Be a man; join the Klan." I have seen it; I have been there. "There is something in the region," says Williams, "something in the blood and culture that fosters the intuition of something almost too incredible and shocking to talk about." Williams goes on to defend what he calls his "crazy people doing terrible things" as being the external symbols of the inward, brooding reality. Thus the terror that he has always felt as characteristic of the universe is particularly accessible in his Southern dramas. It all fits: in Williams' world man is a victim, and the South is a proper stage for the drama.

A third major theme, and the last I will discuss, is that of human isolation. "Each of us," he has written, "is sentenced to solitary confinement in our own skins for life." Perhaps Williams overstates this dilemma, but who has not experienced the feeling of not getting through to others? And is not that the reason we hear so much talk about the problems and breakdowns of *communication*. Now the word "communication" is one I particularly dislike, because it seems to be a pretentious, empty word, as we generally use it. Just as the word "tolerance" has built into it the connotations of superiority and gratuitously withheld power over others, the word "communication" often implies negative connotations for me, for example that we pay attention to the tricks of language, learn the rules, the proper signals, and we will somehow get the message. The image the word always raises for me is of two men desperately signalling to each other by semaphor across a wide expanse of water, while the ships plough past and away from each other, and the two men continue to wave their flags: small, smaller, smaller, smallest . . . tiny. . . . Of course we *can* reach each other, but the trick is a poetic trick; it requires a lyrical and imaginative use of language, an invention of image and symbol driven by the inner necessity to be true to what one feels and believes, and the desire to share it. What we feel is sometimes shocking, of course—and to risk sharing it requires a rare candor and courage. Better the dead, thick skin of formula language, of cliché; better to obscure and generalize than to risk being misunderstood once again, to risk the ridicule of our exposed doubts, ambivalencies, insecurities and terrors. "How are you?" "How *are* you?" "How are *you*?" we are asked. Do I dare disturb the universe? "Fine!" I say, you say, we say, killing the truth, gagging the poems in us, that might say *how we are!* So we learn to *communicate* instead, to make many noises, while the heart pulses in silence like a star in space.

In an essay called "Person to Person," Williams defines his personal lyricism in his plays as: "The outcry of prisoner to prisoner from the cell in solitary where each is confined for the duration of life." Life, he goes on to say,

> is a lonely idea, a lonely condition, so terrifying to think
> of that we usually don't. And so we talk to each other,
> write and wire each other, call each other short and long
> distance across land and sea, clasp hands with each other
> at meeting and parting, fight each other and even destroy
> each other because of this always somewhat thwarted
> effort to break through walls to each other.

Now a play may be considered as a strategic juxtaposition of crucial moments by which meaning may be discovered, a snare for the truth of human experience. In his plays Williams catches his characters at moments most revealing of their lives and at an extremity of feeling that compels them to poetic statement and action. The interior life of his character is forced into vice, as it were, by the pressure of the scenes, and his language at such moments becomes the sound of his agony, his joy, his turmoil, his liberation. The *rest* is *communication*. Poetry speaks to what we are, to what we feel and believe; it rattles the bars of our cells; it breaks that lock; it rips down the walls. The characters in Williams' plays are lonely, alienated, incarcerated; their beauty and human problems shrouded in the language of communication, until those high moments that demand eloquence. Thus the real interest for the audience of lyrical drama is not the plot, not how the play will "turn out" as is said, but the moment when the major characters reveal themselves in the full reality of their inner disharmony. That revelation, paradoxically, demands the most harmonious blending of all the elements of the stage: mood, action, costume, lights, music, pantomime, *language*. All the images and languages of drama—for light is a language and music is a language, and the stage position of the characters is a language—all, ALL must shape the living symbol of meaning. Then can the lonely, alienated character break from the closed chrysalis of silence and wing into our imaginations.

In *The Glass Menagerie* Laura is a crippled girl, and she may be taken as a representative of all those characters in Williams' plays, poems and short stories who are also, in some fashion, crippled. She is the symbol of all those sensitive outcasts for whom Williams has the greatest compassion, for he feels their sensitivity dooms them to mutilation. The radiance of such people is often hidden, obscured, usually, until a fantastic (that is, *true*) moment illuminates them. They are like pieces of translucent glass which when touched by light transmit a brief, beautiful glow. Then the moment passes, and the candle that lit the glass for an instant is snuffed out, and the transitory glow of the glass is gone, like the character, into silence, into darkness, into memory, into death. So Williams' world is one of brief, illuminated, illuminating moments when the lonely speak, not only in words, to be sure, but in all the languages of the drama. Through these various languages Williams makes us aware of the loneliness and cosmic silence we usually deny and attempt to defy by the *noise* of *communication*.

I have discussed three basic themes in Williams' work: sexual desire, the presence of evil, and human isolation. They do not exhaust the catalogue, but one will always find them to various degrees in every Williams play. Now I want to move to some larger considerations of his work.

In his introduction to *The Rose Tattoo*, Williams said: "It is, perhaps more than anything else, the *arrest of time* which has taken place in the completed work of art that gives to certain plays their feeling of depth and significance." If there is any doubt still that Williams is a mere panderer to the prurient, then this comment alone should correct the notion that he is anything less than a serious artist. Williams is correct, I think, and in line with the great tradition of Western dramatic art that began with the Greeks, when he sees the play in its final and total meaning as standing outside of time. The dramatic conventions of the Greeks, who put raised shoes under the feet of the actors, and great masks over their heads, and moved them around the stage in ritualistic patterns, these conventions gave to the audience an impression of epic proportions. Those old plays removed the characters from the dimension of time which makes people little and ordinary and inconsequential and fixed the characters into images of universal significance. We seldom use masks or stilts or choral odes in contemporary plays, but the trick is essentially the same one for significant drama, whether it is Williams or Euripides we are considering. Modern drama has taken advantage of our technology and provided the playwright with equipment of which the Greeks never dreamed. But no amount of hardware, lighting equipment and revolving stages can capture the timeless quality of great statements and the *repose* of great drama. Only the poet can do that, and he does not even need the technology to do it. As Williams has remarked, "Snatching the eternal out of the desperately fleeting is the great magic trick of human existence." This "magic trick" asserts our meaning, our reality, our *being* against impermanence, the flux of time, the erosion of our life, and against the threat of *non-being*. Perhaps Blanche Dubois is a lesser figure than Medea, Phedra, Electra and Clytemnaestra, but to my mind she joins the pantheon of impressive female characters, not merely because she is a well-rendered study of a neurotic, driven, ruined, cracked Southern belle, but rather like her Greek ancestors, she makes us see the immense pathos of the fact that life can kill the individual's most personal, elegant, delicate needs, not only in one great dramatic cut of the scythe, but nerve by nerve, cell by cell—our tenuous hold to dignity and sanity snipped, strand by tiny strand. She makes us see the desperate human need for beauty in a world often brutish. A poem by Williams, "Lament for Moths," speaks to this last point, a poem in which Blanche and the moth may be considered as carrying the same symbolic weight.

> A plague has stricken the moths, the moths are dying,
> their bodies are flakes of bronze on the carpets lying.
> Enemies of the delicate everywhere
> have breathed a pestilent mist into the air.
>
> Lament for the velvety moths, for the moths were lovely.
> Often their tender thoughts, for they thought of me,
> eased the neurotic ills that haunt the day.
> Now an invisible evil takes them away.

I move through the shadowy rooms, I cannot be still,
I must find where the treacherous killer is concealed.
Feverishly I search and still they fall
as fragile as ashes broken against a wall.

Now that the plague has taken the moths away,
who will be cooler than curtains against the day,
who will come early and softly to ease my lot
as I move through the shadowy rooms with a troubled heart?

Give them, O mother of moths and mothers of men,
strength to enter the heavy world again,
for delicate were the moths and badly wanted
here in a world by mammoth figures haunted!

From early in his career Williams seemed instinctively to understand that the essence of great drama is to serve a cathartic and ritualistic function at the same time that it amuses, amazes, captivates and enchants an audience by its usual devices. For the play to move us deeply, we need to feel that we have seen and learned something significant, not been merely diverted for a few hours. The great play has somehow decoded and revealed a little of the mystery of life. We are moved and sobered, and yet, somehow, relieved and satisfied because the play tells us, through the vision of reality the poet renders, that we are not disassociated, meaningless particles, but part of the great human design, that our tribulations and triumphs are less unique and at the same time more significant than we thought. Great drama and religion—for drama grew out of religious ritual and celebration—share a common purpose: revelation, revelation, revelation.

Williams' natural affinity for archetypes—for the ancient myth and primal human types—enhances the revelatory function of his dramas. Ancient myth tells us that the life force was female, and that as the male principle eventually came to differentiate itself and assert its independence, the female force desperately, often successfully, attempted to reabsorb the male force. From this myth springs the many variations of the "terrible mother," the rapacious, entrapping female, a type rife in Williams' world, and obsessively depicted. Another recurrent type in his work is the scapegoat-victim, a human sacrifice to expiate the transgressions, guilts and misfortunes of the society. This is a dramatic situation at least as old as Oedipus, as old as ancient Greek myth which stretches back beyond Homer, who was remote when Plato was alive. Lately I hear God Himself is dead, and so man finds his ultimate victim to satisfy his ultimate, desperate need to assuage one of his most human features: his instructive guilt. A whole new discussion might be launched on Williams' use of myths and archetypes, but I mean only to suggest it here as further evidence of the richness of some of his plays and to account for the sense of depth with which they render the human scene.

After his two great successes, *The Glass Menagerie* and *Streetcar Named Desire*, Williams expressed a view that gives us further insight into his world. He said:

> Every artist has a basic premise pervading his whole life, and that premise can provide the impulse to everything he creates. For me, that dominating premise has been the need for understanding and tenderness and fortitude among individuals trapped by circumstance.

In play after play Williams speaks to the great Christian myth that we are all fallen creatures, imperfect, fallible and sinful. For Williams, however, this makes us not so much punishable as eligible for each other's compassion. Circumstances and other people, as well as our own needs and ignorance and blindness, make life a hell; and we, in turn, become a feature in the hell of others' lives. Only compassion, Williams argues, can break the iron circumstances, can dispel human solitude. Only by the individual's recognition of himself, not society, as sinner, transgressor and tormentor of others may he attain salvation for himself and be of some help to others.

Williams' world has not so much hero and villian types, but rather is populated by characters in various states of blindness and torment, blundering against each other in the half-light, misreading motives, or, in typical egoistic ignorance and innocence, exploding a character's most delicate and fragile feelings like a glass figure crushed under a mindless heel. It is a world with a lot of jungle in it too, where predatory and rapacious creatures slither and stalk, a world that consumes itself to stay alive. "I have seen the face of God," says one character who has watched the sea-birds tear open the soft bellies of new-born turtles; and Blanche thought there was "God so quickly" when Mitch seemed to offer love and a haven for the woman pushed to the edge of insanity; she is the "moth by mammoth figures haunted!" But there is no guiding, benevolent god in Williams' world. God is people who have learned authentic compassion—not sympathy, pity, offensive sentimentality, which are the counterfeits of compassion—people like Hannah and Shannon who, toward the end of *Night of the Iguana,* cut the captured iguana loose from struggling at the end of its rope. Shannon says: "We are going to play God here tonight; Shannon is going to cut the damn lizard loose."

In the final scene of *Night of the Iguana,* a ninety-seven year old poet recites a poem that he has been struggling to create in the extremity of his age and wisdom. It is a death-bed statement. As you may guess, the poet is always a sympathetic character in Williams' world, in his youth the vital seed-bearer in a sexual sense, in his old age the seed bearer of human wisdom. The poem tells us of the inevitable dissolution of all living things and the need for human compassion and individual courage in the full recognition of our fallibility and our mortality, for man is, in Williams' world, a tarnished angel, and the human chronicle is no longer gold. I do not think it ever was. But when our *communication* is transmuted by the lyrical voice and imagination, there might be some gold in our brief, human chronicle. The poet says:

How calmly does the orange branch
Observe the sky begin to blanch—
Without a cry, without a prayer,
With no betrayal of despair.

Sometime while night obscures the tree
The zenith of its life will be
Gone past forever, and from thence
A second history will commence.

A chronicle no longer gold,
A bargaining with mist and mould,
And finally the broken stem
The plummeting to earth; and then

An intercourse not well designed
For beings of a golden kind
Whose native green must arch above
The earth's obscene, corrupting love.

And still the ripe fruit and the branch
Observe the sky begin to blanch
Without a cry, without a prayer,
With no betrayal of despair.

O Courage, could you not as well
Select a second place to dwell,
Not only in that golden tree
But in the frightened heart of me?

Arthur Miller: Aristotelian Canons in the Twentieth Century Drama

by ALAN A. STAMBUSKY

I

In his essay "Tragedy and the Common Man," which appeared in the New York Times shortly after *Death of a Salesman* opened, Arthur Miller categorically rejects the notion that the common world is below tragedy: "I believe that the common man is as apt a subject for tragedy in its highest sense as kings were."[1]

Miller goes on to posit the idea that a modern tragedy of the common man is at least closely allied to, if not identical with, the ancient Aristotelian concept of the classical tragedy of the noble man.[2] What Miller fails to account for in his theory, however, is that what Aristotle means by "noble man" is something quite different and certainly less literal than Miller intends.

Aristotle describes tragedy as the story of the "noble" man, neither villainous nor perfectly virtuous, who is defeated but not wholly subdued by something too large for him to cope with. Such a story, according to Aristotle, can be recognized by its peculiar effect, which is to purge the soul of man by pity and terror.

Arousal in the spectator of the emotions of pity and fear is for Aristotle essential in determining the choice of a tragic hero. The perfectly blameless character must be considered unsuitable because undeserved suffering causes repulsion, not pity and fear. Tragedy in its pure sense, according to Aristotle, presents the ruin of an individual through whose destruction the order of the world is restored. But there can be no disorder reflected in the perfectly blameless character since he is without fault. Hence, no order could be restored through the destruction of such an individual. Nor can characters of moral depravity fulfill the role of tragic hero: good fortune following bad actions awakens no pity. Nor should the downfall of the complete villain be treated in tragedy: a plot of this kind would satisfy the moral sense but not the aesthetic. Aristotle cannot conceive of a character who is at once morally depraved and aesthetically great.

Instead Aristotle places the ideal tragic hero half-way between these two extremes: "a man *not* pre-eminently virtuous and just, whose misfortune, however, is brought upon him *not* by vice and depravity but by some *error of judgment,* the number of those in the enjoyment of great reputation and prosperity."[3] The ideal protagonist of tragedy, then, says Aristotle, must be a man like ourselves, one who does not possess righteousness and virtue *to perfection,* but whose character is held in high esteem by all. In other words, the tragic character will have the same characteristics possessed by all mankind, but these characteristics will be "larger than life," of greater scope than those displayed by ordinary men: he will be more brave, strong-willed, or magnanimous than ordinary persons.

Nowhere in *The Poetics* does Aristotle limit tragic action to the high-bred character alone, as Miller implies in his essay.[4] Aristotle makes no claim for kings and princes of high temporal station as the *only* fit subjects for tragedy. He predicates tragic action to *any* man of spiritual or moral stature, be he king *or* commoner. Royal blood is *not* the essential requirement. When Aristotle describes the ideal tragic hero as one "of the number of those in the enjoyment of great reputation and prosperity," he means simply that the ideal tragic hero must possess high esteem and good reputation among his fellow men. Even Miller's so-called "common man" may be a tragic hero, provided he be of excellent reputation and have a respected status in his own environs. *Moral* quality rather than actual temporal position in life is what Aristotle demands. Miller makes his mistake in falsely attributing the personal quality of "nobility of character" to those with temporal rank alone. By Miller's standards, therefore, even the "common man" who possesses a high reputation would not be fit material for a tragic hero.

Miller says also that the "tragic flaw" in the traditional protagonist of tragedy is a failing "not peculiar to grand or elevated
characters."[5] Here he quite agrees with Aristotle. But Miller adds:
"nor is it necessarily a weakness."[6] Here Miller parts drastically
from Aristotle, who held that the "flaw" was a deep-seated weakness
or tendency toward evil residing in the depths of the protagonist's
character, in his very soul. This "error" or "frailty" which constitutes
the hero's tragic flaw consists in some moral defect inherent in the
tragic hero's character which leads him, "when the chips are down,"
to consciously and intentionally err in judgment and thereby commit some wrong act. Since the defect of character is personal, that
is, residing in the will—and if the hero is not tainted by a depraved
purpose, then he is personally responsible for his wrong act brought
about by the tragic flaw. When such a character of high moral
repute falls into sin through his own action which is occasioned by
the tragic flaw, pity for his sufferings and fear of a similar calamity
befalling them is transmitted to the audience.

Other elements in Aristotle's and Miller's theories of tragedy
are apropos to a discussion of Miller's major works. A brief summa-
tion of them will facilitate the reader's understanding of: 1. how
the Aristotelian canons are or are not represented in his plays, and
2. how Miller's own theory of tragedy is or is not exemplified therein.

Aristotle's principal requirements for tragedy are:

1. the imitation of a universal action which is applicable
    to the lives of all men and does not merely pertain to
    the existence of one particular isolated individual;
2. a dramatic, not narrative, plot that is at once serious,
    complete, unified, and of a certain magnitude;
3. a tragic hero of high moral character whose downfall
    by virtue of his "tragic flaw" results in a catharsis
    which is dependent upon the arousal of pity and fear;
4. a complex plot involving conflict expressed through
    peripeteia (reversal of circumstances) and *anagnorisis*
    (recognition);
5. with character considered as secondary to plot; and
6. the action expressed in "language with pleasurable
    accessories," either prose or poetry.[7]

Those elements Miller considers to be the essential characteristics of true tragedy in the modern age are:

1. the consequence of a man's total compulsion to evaluate himself justly;
2. this compulsion within the protagonist gives rise to his
insistence upon securing his personal dignity;
3. as a result, the protagonist makes an attempt to gain
his "rightful" position in society;
4. his attempt manifests itself in a total onslaught of the
protagonist against his environment;
5. this total onslaught made by the protagonist creates in
the spectator the terror and fear that is classically
associated with tragedy;
6. such terror and fear derive from the underlying fear
of being displaced, the disaster inherent in being torn
away from our chosen image of what and who we
are in this world; and
7. the hero's "tragic flaw" is his inherent unwillingness
to remain passive in the face of what he conceives to
be a challenge to his dignity, to his image of his
rightful status.[8]

Aristotelian universality is evident in the theme of *All My
Sons*. Miller writes about basic human emotions and inner drives
which are common to all men; he portrays the effects of the conflicts these impulses sometimes cause and their influence over man's
sense of moral responsibility. Self-preservation and propagation of
the species are the two chief drives in human nature. Consequently,
all men possess a tendency to evaluate themselves and their families
above the society of which they are a part; to place their private
welfare before the common good.

Miller individualizes this universal drive through the character of Joe Keller, American war-profiteer. Keller is but one of
many Joe Kellers. He symbolizes Everyman who is devoted to his
family; who, despite himself, may be more concerned with making a
living for his family than with his responsibility towards others.
Concerned with such significant human actions, the play's theme is
serious and profound; also, it possesses that "certain magnitude"
which is proper to high tragedy. What the play lacks, however, is
the necessary unity of action, the complete, well-rounded treatment
which is common in high tragedy. It is simply too involved, its
plot threads overwoven. Thus, all the incidents in the play are not integrated with its theme to express one complete action in the Aris-

totelian sense. This is evident, for example, in the lengthy interplay between the Kellers and Deever when George arrives to "rescue" Ann (II). Some of the long, rambling speeches Keller delivers, in his own behalf and in pseudo-defense of his jailed partner, also contain too much material (I). The same is true of Chris's seemingly "moralistic" speeches to Ann about his past war experiences (I). Miller's attempt here at a tightly woven piece of dramaturgy results instead in obvious over-dramatization of his subject-matter. Ideas pour out of him in an abundance that almost swamps his play and make it awkward and muddy. All My Sons embraces entirely too many discordant elements to give it the complete unity of action for high tragedy.

Again the plot is too contrived to preserve unity of action. Almost every climax Miller sets up just so; with almost split-second timing he solves its entanglements by inserting some artificial device which propels the action forward. For instance, a "slip-of-the-tongue" by the mother (II); a letter from the dead flyer which the partner's daughter produces at the convenient climactic moment (III); and a visit to the prison by the girl's brother who had never before visited his convicted father (I). Miller's use of such contrivances to solve plot complications smacks of the melodramatic. True, exciting action caused by melodrama is employed frequently in high tragedy to highlight external manifestations of struggle within the characters. With All My Sons, however, the melodramatic devices, inserted suddenly, seem to be too mechanical for that function. They are not the natural expression of an internal struggle. Hence, they serve only to detract from the play's unity of action.

Miller's preoccupation with social protest is another factor which makes the plot development too contrived. From the overall tone of All My Sons, Miller seems more concerned with advocating a thesis or some moral lesson than he is with portraying significant actions of characters in relation to one another which makes for truly tragic drama. The play becomes didactic primarily, an end not immediately proper to high tragedy. Thus, the tragic quality of the play is weakened considerably. An example of this is the scene wherein George implies that anyone who makes war profits is just as guilty as those who deliberately made defective equipment (II).

Miller's dialogue in All My Sons does not fulfill Aristotle's canons: it is not in any sense poetic; he writes instead with a familiar, literary, sentimental spring that is alien to the dialogue of high tragedy. Also, there seem to be no musical or rhythmic elements to satisfy the Aristotelian demands for melody or song.

Nor has Miller created in Joe Keller a protagonist of Aristotelian dimension because Keller lacks the essential moral integrity proper to the classical tragic hero. Keller's character in the play is not beyond reproach; he is neither "renowned and prosperous" nor is he held in esteem by his fellow men. Also, his crime has been premeditated; that is, he knows himself to be guilty even before the play begins.

Though Keller has been acquitted by the law of the crime of which he was accused, all the townspeople realize he is guilty. They do not ostracize him for it, however, but give him dubious credit for having been able to outsmart the law. Sue, the Kellers' next-door-neighbor, reveals this outright to Ann (II). Even Keller's wife knows his guilt, although she defends him before the others. Throughout the play, Kate is aware of the wrong which Joe will acknowledge only at the end. Several times she hints at his guilt and once even comes close to admitting it openly before Joe (I).

Keller himself always realizes the personal consequences of his deed. He knows tht he is, in some way, guilty of the young flyers' deaths; he evidences this sense of guilt at several points in the play. Moreover, Keller makes no candid effort at any time to confess his crime or to atone for it; in fact, he makes increased efforts to conceal his guilt. Much of the play's action revolves around Keller's always-present sense of insecurity and attempts to keep discovery from his door (I, II). Although Keller adopts a "noble" manner of acting after he has committed his crime, he does so out of a sense of guilt, trying somehow to convince himself as well as his neighbors that he is innocent. He goes on living the lie, feigning the "good" fellow, the friendly neighbor, big-hearted and kindly, the "martyr" who can carry well the weight of a false accusation.

Consequently, Joe Keller is not the true tragic hero, "whose misfortune is brought upon him by some error of judgment." He is instead a purely melodramatic figure, the morally bad man, whose misfortune is brought upon him by his own vice and depravity; the "extremely bad man—falling from happiness into misery." We are moved neither to pity nor to fear at his downfall. The moral sense may be satisfied, but certainly not the aesthetic sense proper to high tragedy.

Similarly, Keller lacks a tragic flaw in the Aristotelian sense. Since his character is tainted at the outset by his own depraved purpose, Keller's misfortune accordingly is deserved and not brought about by his tragic flaw. If at all, he has succumbed to his weakness prior to the action of the play.

There is some sort of moral default in Keller's character, however, which has a share in his downfall: Keller's family and his business for his family's sake are all-important to him. Keller is guilty of blinding himself to a sense of moral responsibility towards those outside his family circle; it results from his placing self-love and family love above all others. His selfish devotion to family dictates that he must seek everything for Chris and Larry with utter disregard for the welfare of other men's sons. Consequently, although he knows he has acted wrongly, Keller tries to rationalize his moral responsibility out of existence. He tries to justify his action of selling cracked airplane engine cylinders by saying that his only intent was to make money for his family: "Chris . . . Chris, I did it for you, it was a chance and I took it for you . . . when would I have another chance to make something for you? . . . For you, a business for you!" (II). Keller possesses, not the tragic flaw as Aristotle means it, but a sort of "post-factum" intellectual self-justification for his evil deed. It is Keller's own way of escaping his sense of guilt at the realization that he has done what he knows to be inherently wrong. Hence, he does not "deny" his guilt, but intellectually "shakes it off" as being "practical"; he has convinced himself that he has acted like any "practical" American would under similar circumstances.

Keller recognizes the "wrongness" of his act. What he does not realize is the gross enormity of that act and its consequences. Even after his son Chris has discovered his father's crime, Keller does not immediately recognize its magnitude and insists before Kate that what he did, no matter how wrong, he did for his family: "I don't know what you mean! You wanted money, so I made money. What must I be forgiven? You wanted money, didn't you?" (III). At the play's end, however, when he learns the contents of Larry's letter revealing how his son has died hating his father for the deed, Keller finally discerns the enormity of his crime: "What is this if it isn't telling me? Sure, he was my son. But I think to him they were all my sons. And I guess they were, kid . . . I guess they were" III). Here Miller seems to give Keller the tragic insight of the classical tragic hero. But Miller has not given Keller any of the other qualities of moral integrity to make him the complete tragic hero.

Keller actually may have felt his personal guilt so much that he refused in the end to face life with himself. But certainly he does not die as the true tragic hero. Being a morally depraved protagonist, his downfall through suicide comes as a just desert for his wrongdoing. Far from causing the tragic catharsis of pity and fear, Keller's misfortune is not even pathetic. We cannot feel pity or fear or even pathos when the suffering is deserved. Though Miller makes us laugh with and like Joe Keller in the early stages of the play, the utter contemptibleness of his wrong to the army flyers and to his partner prevent us from feeling sorry that Keller takes his own life in the end.

In *All My Sons,* Miller does not adhere closely to his own theory of tragedy. No tragic feeling is experienced at the suicide of Keller. Nor does Keller secure "his sense of personal dignity" thereby. If anything, Keller loses that sense by committing suicide, since he had predicated his dignity on an egocentric obsession with his own importance and that of his family above society. Furthermore, it is questionable whether Keller dies trying to preserve an "ideal image of himself," his chosen image of what and who he was in the world. That "ideal image," it seems, is destroyed at the exact moment he puts a bullet through his brain. He does so, precisely because he realizes his "ideal image" is wrong, that one cannot place self and family above a responsibility to society as a whole. Finally, even if it were clear what Miller means by a "rightful position" in society, Keller could hardly be said to have achieved it. At best, he considered himself above society and, refusing to compromise with it, ended his life. Had he wished to preserve his "rightful position," it is more probable that he would have chosen instead to confess and go to jail for his crime thereby paying his debt of responsibility to society.

In *Death of A Salesman,* Arthur Miller illustrates how a good man can be destroyed by the "wrong dream" of a shallow, materialistic way of life based on false ideals. The theme is certainly universal. There are many men who, to some degree at least, think and act as Willy does by placing emphasis on false values in life and by falling victim to the illusion of "power through personality." Willy represents any man whose illusions have made him incapable of dealing realistically with the problems of everyday life. Moreover, Willy's tragic story exemplifies what happens to one who places little or no emphasis on spiritual values. His spiritual "failure" makes evident by contrast the fact that all men are capable of falling victim, as Willy did, to complete spiritual emptiness.

Although Willy evidences little concern with spiritual values, the play itself contains them. Biff is free of illusion at play's end; he realizes that Willy's "dream" of materialistic success has been false; he recognizes that there are higher values in life (II). Charley, too, unlike Willy, displays throughout the play some insight for the nobler things in life. At the funeral, when Linda wonders why Willy should choose to die when "he only needed a little salary," Charley replies: "No man only needs a little salary."

It is questionable whether *Death of a Salesman* is serious enough and of sufficient magnitude to be considered high tragedy in the Aristotelian sense. According to Aristotle, the action of tragedy to be serious must be profound, both in its subject matter and in its spiritual discernment. It cannot be concerned with the petty and mere commonplace acts of men. Yet the actions of Willy in the play never rise above the petty and mere commonplace. Almost everything Willy does, devoid as it is of any real connotation beyond the purely materialistic, demonstrates a notable absence of serious rational consideration. Willy has based his entire life on a false sense of values. A victim of unrealistic success-worhip, his character never rises above the commonplace to that higher sphere of man's rational nature which is concerned with the serious and profound spiritual problems in life.

Conversely, the character of Biff may seem sufficiently developed to adequately represent this magnitude. Biff's whole world is his father; his hope and trust lie solely in that purely human ideal. When that ideal is shattered in Biff's mind with his realization that Willy's "dream" is false, Biff is freed from the illusion. Biff tells Willy how false his own life has been and what he really is, and implies that he will amend his way of living (II). But *Death of A Salesman* is not the story of Biff Loman, the son; it is that of Willy Loman, the father, a story which does not possess the seriousness of high tragedy. The play also lacks sufficient magnitude for high tragedy. Sophocles and Shakespeare dealt with noble minds and hearts which raised the actions of their heroes above the ordinary. Yet Willy's aimless wanderings of mind and spirit, shrouded as they are in the murky mist of illusion, can hardly be reckoned above the ordinary manner of things human.

There is some evidence of the poetic in certain of the play's passages, notably during "the requiem" where Charley eulogizes Willy. On the whole, however, the dialogue in *Death of A Salesman* seems not poetic enough for high tragedy, since it is expressed in blunt, naturalistic prose after the manner of real-life speech. But the musical background provided by the flute as well as a rhythmical lilt in some of the lines would seem to fulfill the Aristotelian canon for melody or song.

What of Willy Loman's claim to stature as a tragic hero? It is doubtful that Willy posesses the moral integrity or spiritual stature indicated by Aristotle and which Miller himself tells us Willy has. Willy countenances, and encourages his sons to countenance, any form of thievery, negligence, or cheating as long as these immoral acts will aid Biff and Happy toward attaining material success in life. He also passes on to them his own illusory sense of values: Willy lies, never admits himself to be wrong; he is even accused of lying by Biff, who sees through Willy's deceptive character. The fact is emphasized in two striking episodes, the first when Willy encourages his boys to steal sand: "Boys! Go right over to where they're building the apartment house and get some sand. We're gonna rebuild the entire front stoop right now! Watch this, Ben!" (I). Later, when he reminisces about the time Biff discovered him with a prostitute, Willy tries to conceal his adultery by lying: "She's a buyer. Buys for J. H. Simmons. She lives down the hall. They're painting. . . . She sees merchandise in her room and they have to keep it looking just so . . . ." But Biff knows that his father is lying and says so: "Don't you touch me, you—liar! . . . You fake! You phoney little fake! You fake!" (II). Not only is Biff's ideal of his father's goodness destroyed; but Willy Loman's own character is revealed as being devoid of moral integrity. He is guilty on two scores: conscious infidelity to his wife and willful deception of Biff. These are hardly characteristics of the classical tragic hero, a man "of the number of those in the enjoyment of great reputation and prosperity."

Despite this, Willy does have a tragic flaw, though it is doubtful whether he ever really reaches "recognition" of the frailty or weakness in his character. Willy is a self-deluded man who has lost the power to distinguish between reality and the obsesions that dominate his life. He is also basically a dishonest man for whom one god—*popularity*—justifies a multitude of sins. It is in this egocentric sense that Willy posesses a tragic flaw.

Personal causation is responsible primarily for Willy's downfall. He is "self-deluded," that is, personally responsible for his obsession with false values and success worship. His tragic flaw results from a conscious will-act on his part; it is not a mere deficiency in his intellect. He is morally responsible for his "frailty," a responsibility to which mere intellectual deficiency could never blind him. Although society plays some part in Willy's downfall, Miller obviously places the personal causation of Willy in the foreground. Proof of this is Charley, the small businessman, who succeeds as a human being in the play, although his life and values are as thoroughly middle-class as Willy's. Nothing in the play indicates that Willy's choice of a salesman's career was a social or economic necessity. He would have been responsible for his own actions no matter what his profession. By his own admission, Willy is a "self-confessed failure, a broken man." Willy's failure as a man is the cause, rather than the effect, of his economic failure. Moreover, even by his own false standards of conduct, Willy proves to be responsible for his state. Many times he admits that a man should be not merely "liked" but "well-liked." And this implies a sense of responsibility on Willy's part to better his personality, false though the standard be.

Willy's sense of personal responsibility is evident in the scene where he has just returned to reality from another of his reminiscences about the woman in Boston. He discovers Linda mending her stockings. Momentarily, Willy becomes angry with her, remembering that he has seldom been able to buy his own wife a new pair: "I won't have you mending stockings in this house! Now throw them out!" (I). Later, when Biff accuses his father of not facing up to reality, Willy reveals his own feeling of responsiblity for what happens to Biff: "When you're rotting somewhere beside the railroad tracks, remember, and don't you dare blame it on me! . . . . I won't take the rap for this, you hear?" (II).

Certainly, Willy is personally responsible for his acts. Even though he may have felt he "didn't have a chance" or the "system" was against him, his sense of guilt for his own failure as well as Biff's could have caused him to rationalize his way out of an otherwise impossible dilemma. Such personal responsibility, therefore, makes him equally responsible for recognizing and for correcting his tagic flaw. Willy is a victim of society, but he is also his own victim: he has accepted an essentially vulgar and debased as well as false system of values.

Willy's personal responsibility also serves as the efficient cause for the conflict within his character: a moral struggle between the forces of good and evil, made manifest in Willy's concern with what he considers "good"—his own sense of false values, and what he considers "evil"—Biff's realization and insistence that Willy's way of life is wrong. Yet Willy never attains the "recognition" proper to the classic hero; he dies, ignorant of what has befallen him. Blinded by his enthusiasm and the obsessions arising therefrom, Willy cannot realize what should have been self-evident: that Biff cannot play the role Willy desires for him.

Significantly, the climax of the play occurs at the exact moment when Willy fails to achieve tragic insight and even rejects that of Biff. And it results from the same condition which causes the play's inciting incident, Willy's refusal to face up to reality:

> *Biff.*   Pop! I'm a dime a dozen, and so are you!
> *Willy.*   I am not a dime a dozen! I am Willy Loman and
>   you are Biff Loman!
> *Biff.*   I am not a leader of men, Willy, and neither are
>   you . . . Pop! I'm nothing! I'm nothing! Pop.
>   Can't you understand that? (II)

But Willy can't "understand that." He fails to recognize his own flaw as well as Biff's. When Biff breaks down, crying, under the impact of his own tragic insight, Willy is at a loss to understand, and murmers dumbly: "What're you doing? What're you doing? Why is he crying?" (II). Later on, standing over Willy's grave, Biff sees his father's failure to achieve tragic insight: "He never knew who he was." Biff alone arrives at an undestanding of different objectives and a different way of life: "I know who I am, kid," he tells Happy. Biff surmounts his father's attitude in acquiring true self-knowledge. Happy, however, does not reach the same recognition: he will persist in following his father's way.

Willy dies precisely because he cannot live up to his private "dream" of success— being "well-liked." He also dies because he cannot see that Biff is unsuited to his own false mode of life. And he dies without ever being able to cope with his obsession—an unlikely condition for the hero of high tragedy. True tragic exaltation springs from a sense of pity and fear occasioned by the hero's insight. Though Willy never reaches that insight, there is a certain pity caused by observing his downfall. This is so because Willy is a common man like most of us; we feel pity for him and fear for ourselves ever becoming like him. Willy is a sort of suburban Everyman with whom we can readily establish a connection. However, since Willy fails to rise to the recognition which high tragedy affords, the pity and fear occasioned by his downfall cannot be that which is commonly associated with high tragedy. Rather, it is more properly considered pathos exactly because there is lacking the "sufficient enlightenment" of high tragedy. Willy is, in the long run, a pathetic figure to us—no more, no less.

Miller follows closely his theory of tragedy in *Death of A Salesman*. It is the tragedy of a common man—not an exceptional hero. It concerns that common man's refusal to relinquish his ideal of himself as an indispensable and admired person, an independent individual who lives and dies for his shallow "dream." These factors are certainly in line with Miller's theory. Whether that dream is worthy or whether Willy Loman ever fully accomplishes those ends is debatable. But as the protagonist of the play, Willy is at least a logical expression of Miller's theory. Where Miller deviates from his idea of tragedy and the common man, however, is in making Willy an object of pathos rather than of true tragic exaltation, and in giving the play definite pessimistic overtones. For in his theory Miller rejects both pathos and pessimism as not proper to tragedy.

Though modern political parallels may abound in *The Crucible,* they do not answer the question of whether the play's overall appeal is universal and thus suited to high tragedy. The answer lies in understanding whether or not the "historical" characters of Salem are representative of humanity as a genus or merely the victims of one isolated event in American history.

From this aspect, *The Crucible* does possess the universal appeal proper to high tragedy. The accused of Salem need not have died; they could have saved themselves by sacrificing their integrity, by "confessing" to a lie. Though the Salemites were hanged for a crime they did not commit, they nonetheless chose to die for something that was close to them personally as it has been to men of all ages: they died to uphold their sense of moral principle, their own individual integrity. They died for their own credit as human beings; they refused to lie, to say they were witches when they were not. Their fate, therefore, is a human fate. *The Crucible* has universal significance, then, since it is concerned with the internal struggle of one accused Salemite, John Proctor, to maintain his personal integrity and sense of decency in the face of total opposition from without. The parallels are deep in the life of every man.

With such a universal theme, *The Crucible* could have been a serious study possessing the magnitude proper to high tragedy. Yet the "cards are stacked" against Proctor from the outset. Accused of a crime he did not commit, there can be no discerning study of the spiritual struggle within his character. He is defeated before he begins; he cannot cope with and overcome what must even be denied existence. Proctor is the helpless victim of a conflict between the wholly innocent and the wholly guilty.

Although *The Crucible* is told "in the form of action, not narrative," its action is, on the whole, incomplete: the play suffers from the absence of a unified, well-rounded treatment. Obvious melodramatic overtones prevent *The Crucible* from penetrating the surface of its central characters. As does *All My Sons,* the play lacks unity of action, which causes it to fall far below high tragedy: *The Crucible* is too involved. It encompasses more in its action than is called for or is capable of being treated within the play's framework. In fact, Miller never does succeed in drawing together completely his abundant mass of material.

Miller's overly-conscientious concern with dramatic action detracts considerably from his character penetration. The play seldom leaves the plane of cold, intellectual argument to arrive at a deeper understanding of the central characters, John and Elizabeth Proctor, who are affected intimately by the events of the play. Thus Miller denies his audience a really warm, human, and sympathetic contact with his two central figures. Miller seemed so absorbed in the headlong rush of his story line that he even has difficulty finding room for the central characters. As a result, John and Elizabeth are never established as fully rounded characters. Never are they permitted to establish themselves as individuals. Later on in the play, Miller makes some attempt to develop them. A quiet interlude presents the Proctors at home revealing their hopes and misgivings about their own private lives (II). But their home life seems so chilly that the audience is not aroused to much sympathy for them until the final scene. Only then are John and Elizabeth brought together once more to show some of the human warmth and emotion of character Miller might have displayed more effectively earlier in the play. Even the avalanche of events inundating the first act are not fully explored or integrated with his theme. Miller fails to develop such elements as the motives underlying the "inquisition of the witches," the terror of misrule by gossip, the inner anguish of the accused when faced with the madness of their accusers.

Miller appears too concerned with mass hysteria and the lesson of the Salem trials to be entirely successful in bridging the gap between himself and his characters. His central characters seem emotionally moving only in so far as they "state their case" in the play. They are instruments of the action first and human beings with private lives and thoughts at second hand; as such, they follow a predestined pattern of action that is not only unmotivated but unreal. Significantly, the frenetic, muffled uproar of the opening scene betrays any motivation for the accusations which follow. The early moments of *The Crucible* are so intense and full of fire that the dramatic tension which properly should come later on in the play is reduced considerably. One notable exception occurs, however: real melodramatic impact is occasioned in act two when the hysterical girls shriek their witchcraft incantations. Most of the other scenes in the play, though Miller obviously intends them to be dynamic, fail to communicate their inherent explosive power.

As in *All My Sons*, Miller again makes use of certain obvious contrivances in *The Crucible* designed to propel the action forward but which serve only to detract from the play's overall unity. Miller causes the inciting incident to be triggered by the willful action of the demoniacal girl, Abigail Williams: she makes the first accusations against the villagers (I). Similarly, the action is clinched in the third act by Abigail who accuses Proctor of having dealt in witchcraft. Miller also introduces adultery between Abigail and Proctor to motivate Abigail's denunciation of Proctor and Elizabeth, thereby causing Proctor to be placed in his fatal circumstances in the last act. Unity of action is destroyed by offering a purely theatrical device as easy motivation for Proctor's eventual downfall. Moreover, Miller avoids suggesting the supernatural in the play's opening scene. Hence, the children seem more mischievous than hysterical, discrediting somewhat their later persistence aimed at the hanging of their victims.

Little of the poetic graces *The Crucible*. There is some striving after poetry periodically, but Miller does it crudely with obvious attempts at an eloquence he does not have. Also, there are no elements in *The Crucible*—save possibly the fanatical chanting of the "possessed" girls or the "roll" of the death drums at the end— which would seem to satisfy Aristotle's requirements for melody or song.

Proctor can hardly be considered the ideal protagonist of high tragedy. Although he is apparently a "good" man, renowned and prosperous among his fellow Salemites, and one who obviously falls from prosperity to adversity in the play, he is "too good" to be a prototype of the classical tragic hero. Proctor is closer to "pure innocence" than anything else. He has weaknesses, but no faults: he has not committed the crime of which he is accused. Proctor is an unsophisticated farmer with a sound sense of right and wrong, a man of integrity who dies rather than sacrifice that integrity. He does not particularly change or grow in stature within the play. Rather, Proctor is the completely "good man . . . passing from happiness to misery" which Aristotle rejects as the ideal tragic hero.

Proctor does not possess a "tragic flaw" which brings about his downfall. By nature a perfectly "blameless" man, he necessarily lacks the "frailty" or "fault" of character proper to the tragic hero; hence, he cannot possibly fall into misfortune on account of it. Nor does the fact that Miller refers to Proctor as a "sinner" (I) and an infrequent churchgoer (Putnam: "I do not think I saw you at Sabbath meeting since snow flew" [I]) make him any more or less the tragic hero. If anything, it detracts from the high spiritual stature demanded of the tragic hero. Even Proctor's mode of action at the play's climax, when he has a chance to save himself from execution by making a false confession, negates the presence of a tragic flaw in his makeup. Proctor acts with a naiveté uncommon to the tragic hero: he wavers a good deal, fails to understand what is happening, wants only to be left alone with his wife and his farm, considers making a false confession, but finally goes to his death for reasons he cannot clearly define but which are good reasons, mainly that he does not want to implicate others. These are hardly characteristics of the tragic hero acting under the influence of his tragic flaw.

No true "discovery" or "recognition" of his tragic flaw is realized on Proctor's part, since he has none. Miller, however, has claimed some sort of "recognition" for Proctor at the play's climax where Proctor shouts:

Because it is my name! Because I cannot have another
in my life! Because I lie and sign myself to lies! Because
I am not worth the dust on the feet of them that hang!
How may I live without my name? I have given you my
soul; leave me my name! (IV)

According to Miller, "Proctor acts and has to face the consequences of his action. In so doing, he discovers who he is. He is a good man . . . . That's what Proctor means near the end of the play when he talks of his 'name.' He is really speaking about his identity, which he cannot surrender."[9] Miller's idea of discovery is something other than the *anagnorisis* proper to the classical tragic hero, however. More than likely, it is simply the realization on Proctor's part that he must continue to preserve the perfect sense of integrity which has already made him the "blameless" character that he is by choosing to die rather than dishonestly betray his fellow-Salemites.

Moreover, Proctor never acts in the manner of the ideal tragic hero. For three long acts, he is constrained and acted upon by forces from without. Only in the final scene does Proctor assert himself to defy his persecutors. He decides to revoke the false confession he had signed and so goes to his death.[10] Though Proctor abandons his early passivity and does act ultimately, he is still the victim of unconquerable circumstances. There is no possibility for Proctor to overcome the false accusations hurled at him from all sides: he is doomed before he starts. Hence, there can be no choice on his part between good or evil. He is propelled to his doom by forces which he cannot possibly overcome.

Since Proctor is perfectly "blameless," his suffering is completely undeserved. Therefore, no Aristotelian tragic catharsis can follow from his misfortune. Undeserved suffering is neither fear-inspiring nor piteous. According to Aristotle, it is "simply odious." In a qualified sense, however, the misfortune of Proctor, undeserved and completely unjust as it is, does strike the spectator as being pathetic. It may even be enlightening in a melodramatic sense: to see an innocent man die to preserve his sense of integrity and to protect his fellow-men is often an uplifting experience.

Potentially, Reverend Hale, more than Proctor, possesses the qualities of the ideal tragic hero. Hale, in all sincerity, helps precipitate the trials; and he truthfully believes that what he is doing is right. Near the end of the play, when he loses all chance of controlling events, he suddenly realizes that he has been deluded by vicious and stupid beliefs. He clearly recognizes his fault: that he has been instrumental in sending to their deaths people who are not only innocent but also good. He even denounces the court proceedings against Proctor and tries to atone for his guilt by begging Proctor to sign the false confession. Historically, John Proctor is the central character and hero of the Salem witch trials. Actually, however, there is much more of the inherently tragic in the character of Hale, the repentant clergyman.

As in *All My Sons*, Miller fails in *The Crucible* to remain close to his theory of tragedy. Proctor is wholly innocent of the charges of witchcraft made against him. Accused unjustly of a crime he never committed, he cannot be held personally responsible for contributing to his own downfall. Instead, Miller makes society solely responsible for Proctor's tragedy. Therein Miller departs from his own idea of tragedy, which he holds must be a result of both conditions taken together. Consequently, *The Crucible* does not represent the "balanced concept of life" Miller insists upon, but denies Proctor's own validity as a tragic hero, which Miller also demands.

II

A View From the Bridge, After the Fall, and *Incident at Vichy* each make some pretense at employing in modern terms the outward trappings of the Aristotelian canons for high tragedy.[12] In this respect, they are all lesser Miller. Except for *A View from the Bridge* in which Miller makes a final abortive attempt to display the tragedy of the common man in classical terms, each of the plays moves farther and farther away from his earlier dramatic form. In fact, *A View from the Bridge* is the last work to date in which Miller has the tragic hero die either onstage or close by immediately after the play's climactic scene. In *After the Fall,* other people die but the central hero does not; in *Incident at Vichy,* though we may suspect the obvious, we are nonetheless left in doubt by Miller as to the ultimate fate of the play's hero.

All three of the plays mark a turning point in Miller's dramatic art wherein he no longer permits the central character of his play to carry the playwright's ideas within the character; instead, the playwright, in the guise of the central character, now stands outside the play's action and voices his theme directly through his character's comments on the action. Miller's lawyer Alfieri in *A View from the Bridge* is the beginning of this new drift in his dramatic technique and the aristocratic Prince Von Berg in *Incident at Vichy* is not yet the end of it.

In Miller's first and shorter version of *A View from the Bridge,* the external, superficial encumbrances of Greek tragedy are obvious:

its physical setting is largely suggestive of ancient Greece, Alfieri the Sicilian lawyer serves ostensibly as a Greek Chorus and talks in pretentious poetry of the Greek and Sicilian past, there are several antique Greek references, and there is even some stodgey blank verse.

Miller's revised two act version of the play, however, does away with most of the superficial attributes of the first script, retaining only Alfieri as a rather superfluous Chorus and eleminating the obvious Greek references as well as all of the blank verse.

A View from the Bridge is the story of Eddie Carbone, the Brooklyn longshoreman, who cannot allow himself to become conscious of his incestuous love for his niece and thereby brings about his own destruction. The play lacks the universality of high tragedy because its hero Eddie, although a good man basically, is living under the influence of a sick and troubled mind. Thus, Eddie's characterization is more the study of a particular psychiatric case than the study of a noble man besieged by some grave personal guilt for a sin committed and later recognized and atoned for.

Essentially, Eddie is unable to face the truth of the nature of his incestuous love, either by attempting an immoral act or even by considering the possibility that he is repressing an immoral desire. Thus, he is compelled as a last resort into an act which he finds even more despicable: informing on his ward's fiance to the immigration authorities. His only alternative, which is to admit what he does not wish to admit—his own incestuous love for his niece—and by will power to control his passion for her, he does not take. If he had, Eddie might have come closer to possessing the stature of the hero of classical tragedy who often exercises the will power to face up to such circumstances. Instead, Miller has made Eddie more pure obsession than man.

Though the outcome of the play is unrelenting, it never reaches the climax of classic tragedy because Eddie lacks true nobility of motive: he simply yields to brute passion. Here is no classic catharsis of pity and fear, but horror and repulsion. Eddie cannot be the true tragic hero then since he is a perfectly blameless character who, through his own mental obsession, brings down disaster upon himself. Nonetheless, the play is a forceful drama about a decent man who is undone by blind passion and self-ignorance.

Urgent, intense, and hard-breathing, *A View from the Bridge* aspires to tragedy without the equipment to achieve it. The play consistently attempts to live above its emotional and intellectual station. Moreover, it suffers from a basic failure in tragic vision and an insufficiency of language rich enough to support its theme.

As in his previous plays, Miller's dialogue is not poetic here either, at least not to the degree which would seem to qualify it for high tragedy. The dialogue of the first version of the play is cast mainly in prose. For the first time in his plays, however, Miller attempts blank verse to underly what he considers to be an ancient theme: when Alfieri as the Chorus serves as narrator or in scenes of great emotional power between Eddie and others in the play. But it is very bad blank verse: Alfieri's speeches are consciously literary, portentous, and occasionally, even false poetic: "his eyes were like tunnels."

In his second version of the play, however, Miller does away with all the ancient conventions of the first, including the blank verse. Even here his facility with language is limited, however, and the revised version, though it may be more power-packed with naturalistic idiom, still does not qualify for the poetic-prose content which might satisfy this requirement for high tragedy.

Miller does not clearly exemplify his own tragic theory in the play because he is more concerned with Eddie's psychological problem in relation to his own subconscious desire for his niece than he is with Eddie's relationship to the society about him and with the social protest which alienates him from that society. Indeed, there is social protest in the play, but it is not as determined as it is in the earlier plays. Moreover, Miller seems to be moving away from his earlier unyielding emphasis on social protest towards a more limited consideration of the individual psyche of his central character. *A View from the Bridge* may be called the last of the early Miller in the sense that, in structure and in form, he is moving away from the old neighborhood of his earlier plays. His voice becomes thinner dramatically and his people become heavily mythologized and dreamlike in a most un-Aristotelian sense.

This latter fact is quite evident in Miller's next play, *After the Fall.* Miller indicates that the play's action "takes place in the mind, thought, and memory of Quentin," (I), a contemporary man. As a result, however, the play is shapeless, tedious, overwritten, and confused. Not only are Quentin's constant flights of mind mystifying, pseudo-mythological and dreamlike, but Miller's scheme of having characters drift in and out of the action in no apparent sense of order is disturbing. Concerned as it is with the amorphous, self-conscious, self-revelations of Quentin, the play lacks any form, plot, significant action, or forward movement which removes it immediately from the unity of action called for by Aristotle. Instead, Miller guides his hero through time and space from childhood to maturity (*Death of a Salesman* technique) and even casts Quentin in the role of a static oracular Chorus (*A View from the Bridge* carryover) commenting on his own involvement. Thus, the play is a long, three hour dramatized monologue in which Quentin alternately addresses the audience informally and jumps in and out of short scenes that are re-enactments of portions of his life, prompted only by what comes into his head momentarily as he speaks in "stream of consciousness" fashion.

Universality of theme in the Aristotelian sense might have been possible in *After the Fall* had Miller developed his play along different lines. Its theme intensely examines one disappointed man's right to hope in a modern-day world where incredible horror and violence keep re-occurring to make one suspect the progress of the human race. It is the description of one man's adventure in self-discovery, a tormented but intellectualized quest for self-justification, a sequence of personal revelations drawn up out of a man's ruthless self-examination. Ideally, then, Quentin's life experience could be typical of his own generation's life experience: he has within him a number of nagging conflicts that are universally felt in our times. In this sense, his experience could have been universalized into a modern day parable of guilt and innocence.

In point of fact, however, Miller's structural treatment of the play's theme denies it that universality. At most, *After the Fall* reveals but a self-conscious pretense at striking out for universal meaning. Miller's whole purpose in the play, aside from its obvious biographical content, is to absolve Quentin of any responsibility for anything that happens to others. Thus, throughout the play Quentin is constantly and everywhere searching for a self-vindication, a justification of his own innocence, an "escaping" of any responsibility or guilt for his own actions or the actions of others. Thus, in the most blatant and harshly cruel scene in the play, when his addict second wife charges him with some sort of responsibility for something, for anything, Quentin ingenuously preserves his innocence by not taking her sleeping pills away from her. For Quentin, that leaves all the guilt with her—where it belongs.

Miller is not questioning the reality of guilt here, only who possesses it; the others are guilty, only Quentin is innocent. Miller is right in a universal sense to note the sure existence of people like

Quentin who cannot accept the reality of others. But he has erred defending, through Quentin, the escapism, the false innocence, of people like Quentin. Not all those in this world who cannot accept the reality of others will make excuses for their own mode of living, their own lack of responsibility, their own presence of guilt, as Quentin does. Some will face up to their own inadequacies in this regard and strive to correct them.

Quentin is not a tragic hero by any criteria, much less Aristotelian standards. He is not a man of profound, complex urges and views. He is shallow and illogical in his reasoning, vain and cold in emotional nature, disdainful of the human race, incapable of giving himself to others; he is insincere and selfish, high on self-esteem, low on self-analysis. Moreover, Quentin is out-and-out dishonest. "You've got to start facing the consequences of your actions," he says (II). But he never lives by that precept: he shows little remorse for abandoning his first wife and child, or for leaving his second in mortal peril, whether or not she could have been saved from suicide. Such ignoring of one's duty to his fellowman is not characteristic of the classical tragic hero.

Moreover, Quentin reaches no sort of tragic recognition in the play stemming from the unresolved conflicts in his soul: there is no true confrontation at any time and no movement from confrontation to understanding. "Maybe it's not enough—to know yourself. Or maybe its too much," he wonders (I). With such a *modus operandi* governing his actions, Quentin is incapable of being the heroic center of any play, not only classical high tragedy.

Once more, as in most of the plays, Miller's dialogue is nonpoetic in *After the Fall*, thus failing to fulfill this Aristotelian canon. Whether or not Miller follows his own tragic theory in *After the Fall* is hard to judge, precisely because with this play Miller seems to be continuing the move he began in *A View from the Bridge* away from his earlier thoughts on tragedy. Here he is no longer concerned primarily with social protest and the common man's immediate concern with his status and "his name" in society. Miller has progressed a large step further toward man's consideration of his own innocence and guilt in the world despite any social ramifications which may be inherent in his particular economic status in society—which was the keynote of his earlier dramas. In one sense at least, ideologically, this new move of Miller's indicates a larger vision, a broadening influence, a definite improvement in his aesthetic outlook as a playwright. Structurally, however,

Miller has failed in *After the Fall* to compose a completely viable dramatic work in the tragic sense.

Incident at Vichy, Miller's latest work, is little more than a searching, illustrated essay, a didactic moral lecture on guilt and responsibility as it concerns the mass murder of European Jewry by the Nazis. It reflects an even further move of Miller as a writer away from the social protest commitment of the individual common man of the earlier plays. In fact, Miller has come almost full circle as a dramatist with this play; at least he has progressed to a dramatic pole which lies at the farthest extreme from his "tragedy of the common man." Ironically enough, the central character of *Incident at Vichy* is not only a common man, he is an Austrian Prince by the name of Von Berg who possesses not only the nobility of character of the classical tragic hero but his nobility of rank as well. These are but shadows of a resemblance to ancient tragedy, however, and neither the character of Von Berg nor the development of the play give any indication that Miller was attempting to continue his earlier tragic theory here.

Miller's particular strength as a dramatist lies in his understanding of and compassion for human beings in their most personal relationships—with the members of their families or with themselves. The essential dramatic conflict in his plays, except for the ponderous *A Memory of Two Mondays* and the morally didactic *Incident at Vichy* is familial. Immediately engrossing are the conflict of father and son in *All My Sons* and *Death of A Salesman* and the triangles of *The Crucible, A View from the Bridge,* and *After the Fall.* And Miller's real virtue as a playwright is his ability to uncover with consummate power the deepest emotions of his characters in dramatic situations.

Miller's weakness as a playwright rests primarily in the extreme intellectualism he finds himself expressing almost without realizing it. This is precisely because his own restless social consciousness and indignation, which are part and parcel of his personality and past experience as an individual, force him to employ the play form as a vehicle for his social protest. Moreover, he attempts to make his preachments palatable by couching them in the uncomfortable coverings of a "modern" concept of tragedy of the common man.

As a theorist, Miller's most glaring fault is that he misconstrues the classical concept of tragedy in his abortive attempts to derive classical connotations from his tragedy of the common man. In his eyes, a "modern" as opposed to an "ancient" tragedy should deal with the problems of society rather than with fate as the force which helps defeat the hero. For tragedy in the classical sense insists that the universe rather than society is the ultimate cause of the human predicament. Understood thus, however, the hero of tragedy cannot be a "little man" as the heroes of Miller invariably are. He must be rather a "great" man who somehow represents an intimation at least of the nobility of which human nature is capable.

Miller may never reach the exalted heights of tragedy that the ancients did. But the powerful effect of his major serious dramas so far upon contemporary American and foreign audiences has revealed some of that same largeness of vision and the certain sense of fatality common to classical high tragedy. In this one respect, that he believes in the essential worth and dignity of man, Arthur Miller now is closer to the ancient tragic concept than any of his leading American contemporaries.

FOOTNOTES

1 Arthur Miller, "Tragedy and the Common Man," *The New York Times,* February 27, 1949, Section II, p. 1.

2 In his "Introduction to the Collected Plays," Miller redefines his earlier position on tragedy by attempting to clarify and, in some instances, even to alter certain statements he made in the original essay. It seems to me, however, that he has failed to establish any new insights on the matter, save perhaps to reinforce the already widely acknowledged critical opinion that Miller quite often takes as literal that which is not always meant to be interpreted literally. As in his plays, Miller is hard pressed here to see beyond the purely literal connotations of the classical tragic concept. Moreover, the substance and tone of his remarks are clearly defensive (as they are not in the original essay) and betray a further desire on his part to rationalize most of the critical objections to his theory which he had not foreseen some eight years previously. Finally, since all of the plays from *All My Sons* through *A View From the Bridge* ostensibly were written under the influence of his earlier thought processes as expressed in the original essay, this later attempt by Miller to postulate *post-factum* premises about his earlier works seems *invalid.* Thus, the original essay, in my opinion, is the more accurate (and certainly the most reliable) statement of Miller's theory of tragedy. See: *Arthur Miller's Collected Plays* (New York, 1957), pp. 3-55.

3 Aristotle, *The Poetics,* trans. Ingram Bywater (Oxford, 1920), p. 50.

4 "Tragedy and the Common Man."

5 *Ibid.*

6 *Ibid.*

7 *The Poetics, passim.*

8 "Tragedy and the Common Man."

9 Miller, cited by Henry Hewes, "Broadway Postscript," *The Saturday Review of Literature,* January 31, 1953, p. 25.

10 This might well be construed as another fault in Miller's approach to the play. For three long acts he tells the story of a completely helpless and persecuted man. Then, in the final act, Miller does a turnabout and gives his

play all the trappings of a man (Hale) who makes a vital decision in his life. It is almost a complete new play, a play-within-a-play.

11 "Tragedy and the Common Man."

12 Miller's other published dramatic works to date—*A Memory of Two Mondays, The Misfits,* and his adaptation of *An Enemy of the People*—I do not consider to be within the scope of this essay. The first, a short "mood" piece only, has no central tragic hero or any other classical similarities; the second is essentially a "cinema-novel"; and the third, merely a re-working of the Ibsen original.

13 There is little, if any, substantive difference between the original one-act version of the play produced in New York (1955) and the longer two-act script (20 additional minutes of dialogue) prepared by Miller for a London production in 1956. Though the additional material is obvious to a fault, the later work only serves to dilute the more self-conscious tragic allusions and make the Chorus character of Alfieri superfluous.

Three Verse Playwrights
and the American Fifties

by DONNA GERSTENBERGER

Verse drama in contemporary theater seems somehow to be a perverse form of creation. In a time in which the failure of communication has become a cliché, in which the portrayal of a distrust in the adequacy of language to convey meaning has reached a fine art, nothing seems less realistic or reasonable than the creation of a verse play. Certainly, within the "modern" context verse may be admitted to the theater for special effect, usually for the purposes of alienation and estrangement as in Brecht's plays or in the verse of the English translation of *Marat/Sade*. Such use of verse seems acceptable to tough-minded moderns, who can no longer be content with the limitations of the naturalism and realism of the theater in the first third of the twentieth century. Yet within the context of the modern theater, verse playwrights persist in writing another kind of verse play—a verse drama in which alienation of the audience is not the *raison d'etre* for the presence of the verse line. The canon of drama in English verse grows with the century, and it is of these plays that the English writer, John Wain, raises the bemused and disbelieving question, "Why Write Verse Drama?"[1]

In the United States the persistence of a verse drama seems expecially perverse, even more so than in the general context in

117

which Mr. Wain asks his unanswerable question. Unlike the other nations which have contributed to the tradition of the Western theater, the United States has never experienced a period in which verse has been an important influence on the stage, and the number of verse dramatists writing for the stage has never been large. The problem of the lack of a theater for the verse playwright's efforts has been a serious one in the United States. Yet without a tradition or a stage, the production of American verse drama has been continual, although all too often plays in verse have been fortunate to find single performances for special audiences dedicated to the "arts" or have been useful primarily in rounding out the "Collected Poems" of the author. No American playwright of verse plays has had the luxury of an Abbey or Mercury Theatre stage to house his work.

Whatever the state of the American theater in general, the state of the American verse theater is not a healthy one, nor has it ever been. Moments of promise, such as those created by the Poets' Theatre at Cambridge, Mass., have not been long enough sustained to create a substantial and healthy body of verse drama, and the few American verse playwrights to achieve any stature have left serious critics somehow even more less-than-satisfied than critics habitually are.

In fact, confronting the canon of recent American verse drama, critics tend to take uncomfortable sides, choosing either the popularized achievement of playwright Maxwell Anderson or the more special achievement of the poet Archibald MacLeish. Having granted the fact that T. S. Eliot's verse drama clearly belongs within a British context, the ease with which the contest is narrowed to these two remaining writers says something about the production of verse drama in the United States today, and the choice one makes between the leading contenders says a great deal about the concept one holds of verse as a dramatic possibility.

The principal argument in Anderson's favor seems to be that he has written plays in verse which have been consistently successful with conventional audiences and that he has made his way as a playwright within something approaching the mainstream of the American theater (for such an argument, see Joseph Wood Krutch's assessment of Anderson in *American Drama Since* 1918 [New York, 1957]). MacLeish, on the other hand, like most other American writers of verse dramas, is essentially a *poet* writing verse for the stage. This argument can be turned around, however, and the opposite conclusion may be drawn: that precisely because Anderson has worked successfully in the mainstream of the theater, he has accepted the stereotyped conventions about verse drama which his audience also shares; the result is a series of clichés (costume dramas with "costume" verse) which have nothing "modern" about them. As Krutch points out in his largely generous and positive survey of Anderson's work, *Winterset*, Anderson's most notable (if somewhat marginal) departure from the easy expectations of the audience of verse theater, met with less than the usual Anderson popular success. The realistic mainstream of the modern theater has long said that verse drama, written for its own sake, must be relegated to a romantic world which is carefully removed from the real world, that its province is at best a backwash or an eddy in the stream of time.

It is not surprising, then, that without a theater, verse dramatists in the United States who have not been willing to settle for the conventional expectations for the use of verse lack any sustained community of effort, nor is it surprising that since most verse dramatists since Shakespeare have been poets first of all, the lack of a theater encourages a tendency toward verse plays for the anthology.

The situation of verse dramas in the 1950's (to take a better than average decade for verse in the American theater) was typical in the sense that the experimental work was being done by poets. The situation was *not* typical, however, in that the Poets' Theatre at Cambridge and the efforts of the Harvard University Press made the atmosphere seem more receptive than usual, made an audience for verse drama in America seem almost a reality. The decade became positively unusual, however, with the popular success of Archibald MacLeish's *J. B.*, the first play by an American playwright to follow Eliot's experimental verse plays to a relatively successful American box office.

Although *J. B.* offered the first substantial challenge to its best American rival, *Winterset*, its preeminence should not obscure the fact that in the fifties other verse dramas were being written by MacLeish and other poets, and that for them the situation was very much the usual one.

A verse play published the same year as *J. B.*, Djuna Barnes' *The Antiphon*, is an interesting case in point. Although the play was enthusiastically reviewed in the *London Times Literary Supplement* as if it were a *poem*, the play is almost wholly unknown. Miss Barnes had contributed three one-act plays to the Provincetown Players during the early years of the twenties, but these plays and

The Antiphon have in no way altered the fact that her reputation as a writer rests upon the poetic prose of her novel, *Nightwood* (1936), which although it has never had a wide popular appeal, has created a sufficient audience for a paperbook reissue by New Directions in 1961. A good part of the responsibility for this situation rests with Miss Barnes herself, for there is in the plays none of that sense of total coherence which marks her poetic novel. To the audience which has received *Nightwood* with admiration, Miss Barnes' long play in verse seems a strange concoction: in subject it is wholly modern, but in conception and execution no more modern than Maxwell Anderson's period pieces in verse.

The Antiphon is set in 1939 (during the war) in the English ancestral halls of the Burley family, and the exterior reminders of a world at war become a metaphor for the interior war within the characters as well as between the sexes and between generations. The play seems to owe a strong debt to W. B. Yeats' *Purgatory* in particular and to many of Yeats' other plays in general (*e.g., The Player Queen*). As in *Purgatory,* the scene of Barnes' play is a compelled if somewhat unwilling return to the ancestral home, the place where many of the difficulties of the present were begot. And as in Yeats' play, much of the present action seems to be defined by a sexual conflict in the past arising from the indignities suffered by an aristocratic mother from a pleasure-loving father (who is, in both cases, of a lower class—in Yeats' play, a groom; in Barnes', an American). The past in both plays provides the source of a neurotic sexual hatred in the present, and both end with death that falls short of resolution.

Yet Yeats' fine play, one of the last on which he worked after some forty years' experimentation in an actual theatrical experience, is a *modern* verse drama, a play in which verse, image, language, action, and subject cohere and support each other as in the best modern poems, while Miss Barnes' play, in spite of its self-conscious modern concern with the relationship of sex and identity is in its trappings, its language, and its verse forms a kind of imitation Elizabethan-Jacobean. It is as if nothing had happened to verse drama for three centuries.

The meaning of the title *The Antiphon* unfortunately describes the movement of the play, although the drama implicit in much liturgical chanting is lacking. Lionel Abel in his essay on *The Antiphon* (*Metatheatre,* New York: 1963, pp. 116 ff.) is accurate in his indictment of the play as a dramatic vehicle:

The Antiphon is a perfect example of what is wrong with
[verse drama]. You get the impression that each character
is trying to make a poem of his or her feelings; no one is
swept into speech by action or emotion. Now who wants
to go to the theatre to watch people writing poetry? . . .
One result is that the characters scarcely talk to each
other. Each one is intent on subtilizing and distilling his
own thought and feeling into a verse expression adequate
to the author's norms of rhetoric, and these are not at all
dramatic norms. The result: there is no dialogue in any
proper sense of the term in this play, and the words
spoken by any one character have scarcely any effect on
the others. It is as if the real action lay in the production
of words, poetic words, and as if each character was too
exhausted by this effort to listen to what the others have
to say.

The truth of Abel's assertion is not obscured by the pageantry
of the play (Miranda and Jack Blow, two of the main characters,
are in theatrical dress of another century, and Jack is further dis-
guised, for he is the lost son and brother of the family), although the
dress of the characters and the setting of the stage seem more in
keeping with the verse of the play than with the use of the World
War II setting. Even though the attitudes of the characters are modern, the verse itself makes no pretense of being the speech of real
people in the modern world. It is full of archaisms, elaborate con-
ceits, involuted descriptions, and Elizabethan phrasing, to say
nothing of its persistent blank verse rhythms. The lines beginning
the play, for example, transport the audience into an Elizabethan
expectation:

Here's a rip in nature; here's gross quiet,
Here's cloistered waste;
Here's rudeness once was home.

. . . .

There's no circulation in the theme . . .
The very fad of being's stopped.

and the character Jack Blow "Coachman" is, through much of the
play, a foil and comic relief character who would seem more at
home on the stage of another time, another convention.

Barnes' cautionary note to the play insists that the real action
of the play is in the duel of wills between Miranda and her mother
Augusta, which is, according to the author, "in hiatus." The dif-

ficulty of this conception for dramatic presentation is that the passion and feeling of the play are lost in the intensity and difficulty of the verse, and what external action there is always carries with it the sense that it is an afterthought. [Author: "My word, this *is* a play. I've got to make the characters move about while they talk. I'll have the brothers (fiftyish) rough up their mother and sister. I'll have them take a whip and make the eighty-year old mother dance." She does].

What becomes obvious from reading *The Antiphon* is the failure which results when the verse dramatist has no sense of the possibilities of his craft in its dramatic dimension, when he has accepted the notion that the proper use for verse in the theater is intensity and that, conversely, intensity is automatically conferred by the use of verse.

Whatever the failures of *The Antiphon,* the play does attempt to use verse to describe an intensely personal experience, a use which is a departure from the conventional subject matter of the great majority of recent dramas in English verse, which seem, with a few notable exceptions, to have taken two themes as special province: politics and religion. One of the many preconceptions relating to verse drama apparently is that the use of verse is tied to the public or ritual world. Verse, it would seem, is the proper language for such subjects in the modern world. Perhaps the difficulty which seems inherent in developing interior character in verse plays has led to an emphasis on public or exterior worlds. Perhaps the more pervasive notion that religious experience is difficult to talk about within the realistic context of the modern world has relegated religious subjects to the verse play in an unconscious pandering to the conventional notion that verse drama by definition is of an unrealistic world.

Another play of the fifties to use verse to examine the immediate private experience is Archibald MacLeish's *This Music Crept by Me Upon the Waters,* the first play to be published in the Poets' Theatre Series of the Harvard University Press. This play marks the abandonment of MacLeish's earlier hope that radio would provide the imagination-centered audience to make possible a living verse drama in the United States. After the publication of *The Trojan Horse,* a verse play written in reaction to the political hysteria of the time, MacLeish gave up the attempt to reach the wide American audience radio had promised but failed to deliver for drama in verse. *This Music Crept by Me Upon the Waters* received, according to MacLeish's Foreword to the play, two different receptions which confirmed his ideas about American audiences. In England the BBC Third Program had made the play available to a large and imaginative public which was receptive to the spoken word as a source of total creation. In the United States, on the other hand, the audience for the play was to be found only in The Poets' Theatre in Cambridge, Mass.—a small, select audience, willing to make possible the staging of verse dramas for which there seemed at that moment small demand in the United States.

In its rather fragile way, *This Music* is reminiscent of Eliot's *The Family Reunion* as MacLeish explores the inner lives of his characters, who, when exposed to a sudden, almost-unbearable natural beauty, confront the emptiness and slow waste of their lives. Although the scene of the play is as special as the mysterious beauty which appears on the sea (the play is set in the Antilles), the characters on this enchanted isle seem very much to be real people who want their dinner, their drinks, and their identities confirmed by their proper military ranks. Even the more sensitive characters, not wholly deadened by modern life, are defined. There is Chuck who has planted palms so that the moon will be precisely framed by their fronds: "Some day this garden will be wonderful/ You wait! Another year. Two years." There is his wife who knows wonder and beauty are now, not to be captured by two years' distant planning: "Why wait? Why not delight in it now?"

The never-never land atmosphere of setting and experience which MacLeish develops in *This Music* is not the usual cliché of nineteenth-century verse drama; it is instead a metaphor for the ineffable and indefinable moment of illumination which may occur in human experience. And this atmosphere, captured so well by the play, is tied to and defined by the ordinary world, the world which none of them finally can escape. This experience in staging a world that seems at once remote and wonderful and at the same time immediately human served MacLeish as an apprenticeship for his accomplishment in *J. B.,* a play which was to follow in a matter of years and surprise an American audience into existence for a verse play. The extent to which MacLeish had mastered his craft is evidenced by the fact that, although MacLeish is telling the most ancient of stories, the world of *J. B.* seems more relevant than that of *This Music* while preserving the same double sense of timelessness and immediacy.

MacLeish's central story of the sufferings of the latter-day Job is set within a circus-like frame, which contains Nickles (Old Nick-Satan) and Mr. Zuss (Zeus-God). The setting is reminiscent of that of MacLeish's parodic poem, *"The End of the World,"* although the particular world of *J. B.* insists on beginning again. Nickles and Mr. Zuss are former actors, who are not content with their life-roles as circus vendors; unlike *J. B.*, they must kick against their fall from fortune. The scene in the "enormous circus tent" is ambiguous: the now-unused trappings of this "side show" have religious overtones, from the *seven* straight chairs MacLeish specifies to the "clothes that have the look of vestments of many churches." The action of the play confirms the irrelevance of the side show that religions have made of man's relationship to God.

MacLeish's frame works as a part of his total statement, and *J. B.* succeeds precisely because MacLeish has found a means of *dramatizing* his material. He has found a dramatic equivalent for the poetry of his play. Zuss and Nickles, playing their part in the Job story, become a chorus involved in the meaning of the action—not as God-players but as all men are involved in the significance of Job's story. The use of God and Satan masks, the projection of the two actors' shadows larger than life, and finally the voice of God from without are dramatically and poetically convincing. The poetry here is not the poetry of language alone, but rather the joining of verse to the *poesie de theatre* of Cocteau.

Within this compelling framework, the story of the one perfect and upright man is translated into the modern story of the successful businessman, *J. B.*

It is this central core of the play, J. B.'s testing and response, which has drawn the most adverse criticism from readers of the text. An interesting aspect of this kind of criticism is that it approaches the story of J. B. as if it were the whole play, and this criticism finds the story too banal in MacLeish's rendering, too mechanical in its stripping away of J. B.'s possessions and family, in its piling of horror upon horror until the condition of J. B.'s instruction becomes that of an entire world in ruins. The story, we are told, does not have the force or the instruction of the original. The Critics who so complain that MacLeish has not done a good enough job in staging the Job story have not only failed to conceive of the play as a totality (including Zuss and Nickles and the circus world) but they have also failed to free themselves of their preconceived notions about the meaning of Job's suffering, about the old story of justifying the ways of God to man, to give MacLeish's play a careful hearing.

MacLeish's J. B. is not the Job we have been taught to expect, and it is significant that Mr. Zuss is as unsatisfied with J. B. in the conclusion of the trials as is the devil-advocate Nickles, who goes to J. B. for a special pleading. J. B. has offended Mr. Zuss by understanding, by forgiving:

> The whole creation! And God showed him!
> God stood stooping there to show him!
> Last Orion! Least sea shell! . . .
> And what did Job do?
>
> . . . .
>   Then, he *calmed* me!
> Gentled me the way a farmhand
> Gentles a bulging, bulging bull!
> Forgave me! . . .
>   for the world! . . .
>   for everything!

This is the mystery of *J. B.*, MacLeish's Job, that "In spite of all he'd lost and loved/*He* understood and he forgave it!" The conclusion is not the one expected by Mr. Zuss nor is it one that conforms to Sarah's earlier vision of the goodness of the world as something to be *earned* of God.

The answer given by the play is one reminiscent of Ivan Karamazov's conclusion as he also struggles with the problem of justice in an evil universe: "Though I may not believe in the order of the universe, yet I love the sticky little leaves as they open in spring, I love the blue sky, I love some people." This is the final mystery, the irrefutable proof that God *is*: that J. B.—Job, knowing the pain and the loss will begin again because of the evidence of a few leaves on a bough, that J. B., having suffered all, still has compassion toward God, still is willing to blow on the coal of the heart to warm the world again. As Nickles knows, J. B. has been right all along in his sense of life and of man's relationship to God and the universe. The man of the Thanksgiving scene at the beginning of J. B.'s story is the man of the final lines of the play. That this man should suffer so much and be willing to begin again *in spite of the fact* that he knows finally that there is no meaning in the suffering: this is the final mystery and the greatest proof.

MacLeish's mystery is centered in man, and yet the mystery attests to the greatness of God. Man *loves* and the world renews itself—inexplicably, unreasonably, stubbornly. This is more than Mr. Zuss the God-mask can swallow as it has been more than the churches could swallow through all the centuries after Job. The *whole* play contrasts the simplicity of J. B.'s story with the ecclesiastical circus which would bend that story to the ends of the dialogue between the God and the Devil-mask. The simple truth is that, without benefit of clergy, the play ends with J. B. and Sarah and the forsythia beginning again.

While *J. B.* is itself something of a miracle in the canon of American verse dramas, to end this discussion with MacLeish's relative triumph would be to falsify the American experience in this area of artistic creation. For this reason, I wish to extend the examination of American verse playwrights to include the experiences of Richard Eberhart. Although Eberhart is almost wholly unknown as a verse dramatist, he is another American poet who began work in this area in the 30's and produced several pieces for the Poets Theatre in the 50's, including *The Visionary Farms* probably the most ambitious of Eberhart's verse plays. Unlike his earlier verse plays, which consisted largely of dialogue, poetic talk among characters, Eberhart intended *The Visionary Farms* to be a play with a strong plot and complete characterization, an Aristotelian totality the earlier dialogues had not achieved.

Although one must conclude that *The Visionary Farms* falls short of being a play to achieve the stature of MacLeish's *J. B., The Visionary Farms* is distinctive because its subject is typically American. (J. B. and his family also are Americans, but not typically so, for good reason.) Eberhart's play examines the very American will to succeed at any cost, the need to define success in essentially frivolous terms. It is this will and this need which drive Hurricane ("Hurry") Ransome, the creator of the Visionary Farms, to establish a show place home for the world's best poultry (even if its prize-winning roosters have to be improved by a surgical knife). The subject is chickens, and we would expect a comic treatment, but Eberhart sees his play as one with tragic implications.

Ransome's show of success is not unlike that of another American literary hero, Jay Gatsby, for Ransome builds his visionary farms on an unethical substructure, on money embezzled by him in his role of comptroller of a large corporation. Ransome's actions are predictable from the first moment we see him demon-

stating to his Congregational Sunday School class the difference between good and evil by the manipulation of a silver dollar.

> Notice the brightness of this dollar.
> See how clean it is, hard and pure,
> A symbol of the American dream.
> I will drop it in this glass of water.

The dollar in the glass of water remains "Bright, hard, pure and
clean." Then Ransome drops it in a glass of hydrochloric acid.
"See how it is black all over.   Where is its brightness and its clean-
liness?" Souls, of course, like dollars, corrode when immersed in
sin. Ransome is indeed, as his name suggests, a product of a society for which a money-ethic provides its foundations.

There is another theme which is developed in the play that is
a part of the typical American experience: the identification of the
good life as a version of pastoral. The vision as it remains in its
vestigial forms in a world without real frontiers is cheapened and
mechanized but nonetheless tenacious. Ransome's money, stolen
from an industrial source, is plowed into the Farms, and Adam
Fahnstock, the secretary and vice president of the corporation from
which Ransome steals, embodies his success in farms and expansive
lawns and family barbecues. The scene in which Adam Fahnstock
announces to his family that he has been ruined financially by Ransome and that his wife is dying is set in the apple orchard of the
Fahnstock estate, perhaps by way of reminding the audience of the
original Fall or perhaps that modern life can at best be a version of
ruined pastoral. Whatever Eberhart's intention—and it does not
take clear shape in the play—this strange *American* yoking of the
dream of success with the pastoral is present to convince us that
we have at last come upon an American verse dramatist who writes
a verse play with a typically American theme.

Eberhart has also set his play within a frame, in the home of
Robin Everyman, who with his wife and friends, becomes an intellectual chorus for the story of the Visionary Farms. It is at this
point (as well as at others) that *The Visionary Farms* suffers from
comparison wih MacLeish's *J. B.*, for Eberhart's frame, his chorus,
does not operate to inform the whole play as MacLeish's does.
In *The Visionary Farms*, the chorus is never more than a frame.
This failure to conceive a totality which might answer Wain's ques-

tion about "Why verse drama at all?" is the price exacted from poets who are occasional verse dramatists.

A failure harder to understand than the failure of structural conception, is the failure of language which occurs in verse drama as often as not. A competent poet like Eberhart suddenly begins to sound like a man writing an English version of Puccini:

> Suzanne, don't you want to go in the kitchen
> And watch Inga make the strawberry shortcake?
>> SUZANNE
> Yes, Mother.
>> VINE
>> You said Mr. Parker was coming over?
>> FAHNSTOCK
> Roger said he would drop over for a visit.
>> VINE
> We must get the new Victrola fixed.
> I am anxious to hear the new Caruso records.

Eberhart's fairly occasional failures of language in *The Visionary Farms* are at the opposite end of the spectrum from Barnes' involuted and tortured density. Only MacLeish of these three principal verse playwrights of the American 50's seems to have found a convincing middle ground.

The real miracle of American verse drama is the same as that of *J. B.*, simply that it *is*, that in spite of all the failure and frustration, verse dramatists are willing to begin again, to have another go at a form which seems a most difficult and most unreasonable pursuit.

FOOTNOTES

[1]John Wain, "Why Write Verse Drama?" *London Magazine* VII: 1 (January, 1960), 58-63.

What Happens in Who's Afraid...?

by MAX HALPEREN

Everyone seems to be in agreement on two aspects of *Who's Afraid of Virginia Woolf?* First, that the play is brilliant; indeed, though Albee has continued to produce, it remains his best, certainly his most moving, play to date. Second, that it is obscure. There is relatively little agreement on the scope, meaning, and even the action of the play. One reputable critic, generally friendly to Albee, sees the play as "nothing more . . . than a dissection of an extremely ambiguously conceived sick marriage." Thoroughly unfriendly to Albee, another critic has insisted that the play succeeds only in gratifying "an adolescent culture which likes to think of itself as decadent," a remark that at least puts the play in a social context.

A clear understanding of *Who's Afraid* requires, I think, a clear understanding of the plays that preceded it, for Albee was, in all of them, dealing with the same set of themes, even the same set of motifs. In analyzing *Who's Afraid,* then, I intend to provide partial analyses of *Zoo Story, The American Dream,* and *The Death of Bessie Smith.*

As all the interested world knows by now, *Who's Afraid of Virginia Woolf?* deals with an all-night drinking party at the home of a middle-aged history professor, George, and his wife, Martha, daughter of the college president. Their guests are Nick, a young biology teacher, and his wife, Honey, who enlivens the evening by

129

throwing up at least two—and perhaps three—times. Not that the party is otherwise lacking in vigor; to quote George: "it gets pretty bouncy. . . ." Humiliated by Martha time after time, George finally loses control and tries to strangle her; then, rather mysteriously, he dominates the remainder of the play. "We're done with Humiliate the Host," he announces, ". . . and we don't want to play Hump the Hostess, yet . . . not yet . . . so I know what we'll play. . . . We'll play a round of Get the Guests. How about that? How about a little game of Get the Guests?" The game is played by thoroughly humiliating Nick and Honey, after which George "gets" Martha by announcing the death of a make-believe child that he and Martha have created over the years as an imaginary substitute for the child they did not have. And, of course, Nick and Martha do play a round of "Hump the Hostess" — to which George reacts rather strangely to say the least. In and around these games there is much chatter about the historical process and much banter about Nick—a brash, hard, up-and-coming young man—as the wave of the future. If Albee does not intend his play to extend beyond the arena of one very sick marriage, and if all we really have is a play about two manic-depressives whose manic phases happen to coincide, then the playwright has certainly thrown some very smelly red herrings in our path, and we would hate to think so poorly of him.

To Albee, a man obsessed, there is one deadly sin: fear and rejection of some aspect of tangled, moist reality; and escape into the smooth deserts of illusion and indifference—an escape which, as far as Albee is concerned, is its own punishment. One may reject a part of oneself or society, the result is the same: inadequacy, insignificance, confusion of one's role in life. In *The Zoo Story*, two characters, Peter and Jerry, divide the world between them. Placid, middle-aged, middle-classed, Peter sits in the park of a Sunday afternoon on a favorite bench, where he is accosted by Jerry. Though sophisticated, Peter accepts the norms and judgments of his society, and there is no room in that respectable universe for the experience contained in the poor and lonely Jerry, who lives across the hall from a Puerto Rican family and next door to a homosexual. But in his sojourn among society's outcasts, in society's underworld, Jerry has learned something Perry does not know, or has forgotten. For "sometimes," according to Jerry, "a person has to go a very long distance out of his way to come back a short distance correctly." Jerry has come back to an understanding of man's feral nature—his baser instincts, as we have been taught to call them.

And Jerry knows, too, that any genuine communication, any real contact, requires an appeal to the lower as well as the upper being. (If this sounds like D. H. Lawrence—indeed, like half the literature of the twentieth century and a large slice of the nineteenth—we may assume that any mystery in Albee lies in his manner, scarcely in his matter.) But the lower being has been throughly repressed, as it has been in George in *Who's Afraid of Virginia Woolf?* So that Jerry can make contact only by deliberately awakening the slumbering animal in Peter—pushing him, insulting him, slapping him, forcing him to pick up a knife in self-defense. Whereupon, in a rather horrendous scene, Jerry impales himself upon the knife. Between the two animals contact has been established unforgettably. The beast in Peter, and, by implication, the carefully penned "animals" in society at large, can no longer be disowned. Thus George, in *Who's Afraid of Virginia Woolf?* must be prodded and insulted into a murderous attack on Martha before he can achieve wholeness and become effective as a man and as an intellectual.

Placid Peter's counterpart in *The American Dream* is a character known only as Daddy. In the comic parlance of *The American Dream* Daddy is, quite literally, without guts. We are told that he has had a little operation in which they were replaced by tubes, though he has occasional "qualms" and "misgivings" "right around where the stitches were." There is no animal left to be awakened. His world is dominated by Mommy, the demon of the house, who gets what she calls "satisfaction" in throughly meaningless quarrels. "You can't get satisfaction," she tells Daddy; "just try. *I* can get satisfaction, but you can't." Clearly, we are more than a step nearer the emotional caverns of Martha and George, where men and women wander in the half-dark, having forgotten their organic realities, and substituting for that lost knowledge their pathetic, albeit vicious, games. And, in *The American Dream,* just as, in *Who's Afraid of Virginia Woolf?,* an illusive child becomes the primary symbol of that substitution or evasion. Albee seems to have brooded on the theme for some time. We are told that Mommy and Daddy had a child some twenty years ago—a little "bumble of joy"—but the taboos of the genteel, Mommy-dominated world, taboos destructive of genuine affection, individuality, and sensuality, rendered the child spiritless. According to Grandma, "it didn't have a head on its shoulders, it had no guts, it was spineless, its feet were made of clay. . . ." And as the "last straw, it finally gave up and died. . . ." Mommy and Daddy, in other words, cannot stand too much reality;

they have rejected the consequences of ordinary flesh-and-blood behavior. What is left is the current American Dream, a dream personified toward the end of the play by an "almost insultingly good-looking young man" who will do anything for money but who has lost the capacity to feel anything—a blend of Hollywood fantasy and commercial reality. "I have no talents at all," he tells Grandma, "except what you see . . . my person; my body, my face. In every other way I am incomplete, and I must therefore . . . compensate." An ideal, not a person, the clean-cut Hollywood giant who is the American Dream represents the ways in which the American people compensate for their loss of creative vitality, a loss which, in turn, results from their rejection or attempted denial of certain grisly facts of life. There is, as we shall see, a similar denial of life and a similar substitution in *Who's Afraid of Virginia Woolf?*

In *The Death of Bessie Smith,* the compensatory mechanism of rejection and substitution is not suggested symbolically, but installed quite obviously in one of the characters, the Nurse (she has no other name). Bored and frustrated, she screeches: "I am *sick.* I am sick of everything in this hot, stupid, fly-ridden *world.* I am sick of the disparity between things as they are, and as they should be! . . . I am tired . . . I am tired of the truth . . . and I am tired of lying about the truth . . . I am tired of my skin. . . . I WANT OUT!" Her way of getting out is to seize upon a young and weakly idealistic intern, threaten to have him fired because of a passing, and no doubt true, remark on her lack of chastity, and and to turn him into her flunky: ". . . you will be my gallant. We will have things between us a little bit the way I am told things *used* to be. You will *court* me, boy, and you will do it *right!*" For a while the intern acts the gallant, but like Peter and George he is shocked into an awakening —in his case, by the arrival of the corpse of the Negro jazz singer Bessie Smith, who has bled to death because her admission at another white hospital was delayed. The intern defies the nurse; at the end slaps her face. Stunned that her manager should bring a dead Bessie Smith to the hospital, the intern shouts: "WHAT DID YOU EXPECT *ME* TO DO, EH? WHAT WAS *I* SUPPOSED TO DO?" The answer, of course, is nothing for Bessie Smith, and yet everything. The intern has been guilty of the sin of passivity, of acquiescence in a lie; and in this we are a giant step closer to *Who's Afraid of Virginia Woolf?,* for that is precisely George's major sin.

Denial and retreat mark these characters—retreat into complacency by Peter and Daddy, into meaningless domineering by Mommy, into a romanticized past by the Nurse. Certain of them, like the Nurse, are perfectly capable of exerting social and economic pressures in order to have their way. But it is Albee's contention that none of these pressures are worth a man's soul or identity. The intern learns this: "Honey," he tells the Nurse, ". . . you going to fix me? You going to have the mayor throw me out of here on my butt?" Disobeying her, he points out: "Well, honey, whatever it is you're going to do . . . it might as well be now as any other time." *The American Dream* puts it all in the form of an obviously imbalanced equation, Mommy announcing firmly that Daddy must obey her in all things because she is married to him and because he once had his sexual will of her. Daddy, having had his operation, does not rebel. To acquiesce, for personal or social reasons, is to lose a part of oneself, according to Albee, and what has been lost, or repressed, as Peter and George—and for that matter Martha—learn, is not easily redeemed or rediscovered. For the half-man to achieve wholeness, in Albee's world, often requires somthing of an explosion.

Only out of the whole man, the man who accepts body as well as mind, the more savage impulses as well as the civilized matrix that is society, the painful as well as the euphoric, can come genuine love, love that is not sick, neither overly weak nor overly agressive. Otherwise, we get the Mommy-Daddy relationship of *The American Dream,* the George-Martha relationship of *Who's Afraid.* And only out of the whole man can come effective communication, words that create action. Otherwise we have the tepid complacency of Peter, who has intellectual pretensions, or the impotence of George, who claims to be a teacher. *Who's Afraid of Virginia Woolf?* deals both in love and communication—it operates on the emotional and the intellectual level. On one level, the half-man cannot love; on the second level, he cannot lead.

Halfway through *Who's Afraid of Virginia Woolf?* George rediscovers a demonic self he has long repressed, rediscovers it in its most extreme form—the urge to kill—and for the moment he emerges as a whole man. The play changes course, just as George does. For George knows what Jerry learned in *The Zoo Story*—that "neither kindness nor cruelty by themselves, independent of each other, creates any effect beyond themselves; . . . that the two combined, together, at the same time, are the teaching emotion." In words very reminiscent of these, Martha, in Act III of *Who's*

Afraid, speaks of George as one "who tolerates, which is intolerable; who is kind, which is cruel; who understands, which is beyond comprehension. . . ." It is possible to be too kind, too tolerant, and thus not only to become personally ineffectual but to create a female monster by indulging it in all its fantasies and illusions about itself. And this, says Albee, is what the American male, out of real fear and false compassion, has done. In one of the key speeches of the play, near the close of Act II, George tells Martha: ". . . you've taken a new tack, Martha, over the past couple of centuries —or however long it's been I've lived in this house with you—that makes it just too much . . . too much. I don't mind your dirty under-things in public . . . well, I *do* mind, but I've reconciled myself to that . . . but you've moved bag and baggage into your own fantasy world now, and you've started playing variations on your own dis-tortions. . . ." Shortly afterward he tells her, "You're a monster . . . you *are.*"

Indeed she is a monster. She has brayed, cursed, drunk, and fornicated her way through the play. Like the Hollywood giant of *The American Dream* she is incomplete and must, therefore, com-pensate. She lacks any organic, any significant, connection with life, a fact that is embodied for Albee (or disembodied—there are too many negatives here) by her lack of children. It is not simply that she was unable to have them: at the end of Act II, Honey, thoroughly drunk, begins to whimper: "I DON'T WANT . . . ANY CHILDREN . . . I . . . don't . . . want . . . children. I'm afraid! I don't want to hurt. . . ." George recognizes the symptoms much too easily; here is a strong hint that he's been through it all before. And for the moment he is quite compassionate, as he no doubt was to Martha: "I should have known . . . the whole business . . . the headaches . . . the whining. . . ." Honey has been aborting her children, and it seems likely that Martha did too. As a result, Martha has retired into the sterile—and disappointing—world of *The American Dream,* the world of power, both business and sexual power. Employing the values of this world, she can bury her own failures—achieve a kind of triumph—by heaping abuse on George for his failures. In an oddly Oedipal way, in fact, she in-tended George as a kind of compensatory son, for she tried to make him heir to her father's presidency; but George, of course, simply would not do. "So," she tells her guests, "here I am, stuck with this flop . . . this BOG in the History department . . . who's expected to be somebody, not just nobody, some bookworm, some-body who's so damn . . . comtemplative, he can't make anything out

of himself, somebody without . . . guts. . . ." She can also bury her
failure in promiscuity, but even here, George and George's reactions are far more important to her than her affairs. At the end of
Act II and the beginning of Act III, Martha makes love to Nick,
but in the mirror of Nick's mind, she sees little more than a 52-
year-old woman whose attraction lies primarily in her being the
daughter of the college president. Only if George reacts properly
can she become alive sexually. When George refuses to react at all,
Martha becomes unmanageably angry. Futile in her grey world,
Martha can scarcely see or feel herself except by punishing George,
and her punishment gets harder and harder to bear.

Of course, one reason George bears up so well is that Martha's
blows satisfy a need of his own, something Nick implies at the
beginning of Act II and that Martha—to George's horror—states
openly at the end of the Act. For the more of a harridan she is,
the more George can prove to himself and to others that he is trapped.
The more vulgarly childish she is, the more readily he can appear as
the wise, ironic adult. Thus, in speaking of Martha and her vul-
garities, George is at his ironic best; in cutting her down to size,
he adds stature to his own. It is an intricate web of excuse,
evasion, and illusion that George and Martha have woven for each
other, and only they can maintain that web. They need each
other. So that, to repeat, if Martha is a monster, George, by com-
plicity and acquiescence, if not by positive connivance, has helped
create her, until she has become precisely what he calls her: "spoiled,
self-indulgent, willful, dirty-minded, liquor ridden. . . ." The process
is made clear in Act III. There has been another futile attempt by
Martha to escape herself in another pointless infidelity—this time
with Nick—and Martha, as usual, feels let down. Not that we get
any melodrama—she has been through it all before. There is a good
deal of cheerful self-mockery in the little act she puts on: "Deserted!
Abandon-ed! Left out in the cold like an old pussy-cat. HA! Can I
get you a drink, Martha? Why, thank you, George; that's very kind
of you. No, Martha, no; why I'd do anything for you. Would you,
George? Why, I'd do anything for you, too. Would you, Martha?
Why certainly, George. Martha, I've misjudged you. And I've misjudged you, too, George. WHERE IS EVERYBODY!!!" And she is
perfectly aware of Nick's motives: "You didn't chase me around the
kitchen and up the goddamn stairs out of mad, driven passion, did
you now? You were thinking a little bit about your career, weren't

you? Well, you can just houseboy your way up the ladder for a while." When Nick asks Martha, "There's no limit to you, is there?" she replies, very calmly, very surely, "No, baby; none."

And George, when he appears, falls immediately into a pattern of behavior Martha has come to expect. Compassionate George, forgiving George, understanding George has always returned after her more manic scenes and, more or less good-humoredly, picked up the pieces. He brings her a great bouquet of snap-dragons, laughs with her over Nick—cementing the two of them against the very bewildered young man—and then, in one of the oddest scenes of this odd play, George and Martha join in a long and senseless argument as to whether the moon is up or down. Neither goes to the window to look—or to put it another way, both very carefully avoid going to the window, for between them, as both know, reality can become a matter of agreement, and thus the pain of disappointment and frustration may be overcome. No wonder Nick explodes: "Hell, I don't know when you people are lying, or what." "You're damned right!" Martha replies. "You're not supposed to," George adds. Clearly they have played this scene before, and always before they have ended by walking up the stairs, arm and arm. But George has something else in mind for this night—or morning.

On the second level of the play—that dealing with the failure of the American intellectual—George is as passive and as ineffectual as he is on the first. As a historian—that is, as an intellectual and as a teacher—George insists on the responsibility of the individual for his society. He knows that, apart from the individuals that create it, there is no such thing as an inevitable historical process. But as a person—that is, not as an intellectual—he is paralyzed, tolerating and adjusting to a society he despises, as he has tolerated and adjusted to Martha. Even when he speaks his mind, he often adopts the role of the sad clown whom no one need listen to. That, I think, is the point of George's skylarking in Act I. He spins a grandiose fantasy, insisting that Nick, the biologist, is preparing the way for a race of uniformly perfect, test-tube-bred men. History, of course, "will lose its glorious variety and unpredictability. I, and with me the . . . surprise, the multiplexity, the sea changing rhythm of . . . history, will be eliminated." He concludes: "I will not give up things like that. No . . . I won't. I will fight you, young man . . . I will battle you to the death." Obviously, while George is concerned with history's "variety and unpredictability," he scarcely intends to fight anyone. Life is still a matter of "Fun and Games." In Act II, while George supplies bantering references to "historical inevitability," Nick daydreams the step by step climb by which he intends to take over "the whole works": ". . . what I thought I'd do is . . . I'd sort of insinuate myself generally, play around for a while, find all the weak spots. . . ." and turn himself into an inevitability. There would, of course, be no change in the status quo; Nick, the brash young member of the takeover generation, would simply be extending it, thereby extending its life in history. And George, like the American intellectual, responds lightly and ironically and thus, in a real sense, becomes responsible for Nick, as he has been responsible for Martha.

Change comes suddenly, smack in the middle of the play. Up to this point, George has managed, somehow, to survive, to keep himself under control.He has been humiliated by Martha, ridiculed by Nick. But theirs, after all, is a foreign code of conscience. Inwardly, in his private world, George is at rest. The nature of that private world is suggested or imaged by a story George tells Nick early in Act II, the story of a little boy who kills his mother in a shooting accident, kills his father in an automobile accident, and then goes insane. And "for these thirty years," George asserts, the boy "has . . . not uttered . . . one . . . sound." Is George the little boy? The play raises the question but very carefully fails to answer it; for all answers are equally possible in the unreal world of George and Martha. Certainly it seems more than likely that George is talking about himself. But whatever the answer, the point of the story seems clear enough: in an absurd world, the only adequate response seems to be immobility; to act may be to hurt—indeed, to kill. The story clearly has immense emotional significance for George; like the little boy, he has, for some thirty years, feared and repressed his more feral impulses. And in telling his story to Nick, George exerts all of his considerable skill as a storyteller to make Nick sympathize with the plight of the little boy, and, by proxy, with George. Left alone to the quiet employment of his own devices, George—and by extension the American intellectual —can be quite effective. He does get Nick to sympathize.

But now Martha, losing all sense of limit, invades George's private world; she recites the story of the little boy her way, and, of course, scarcely gives it a sympathetic rendering. As she and Nick dance in what Albee terms the *Walpurgisnacht,* she tells of a novel George has written but which her father insisted not be published. It was, of course, a novel about the little boy who killed both his parents. Containing himself until the very last—for only then is his world finally invaded, all defenses down—George gives way when Martha reveals his reply to her father: "this isn't a novel at all . . . this is the truth . . . this really happened . . . TO ME!" At this point George's inner world is exposed to the savagely unsympathetic view of Martha and Nick, and, as in Sartre's *No Exit,* "Hell is other people." The tale, significant to George because of his rationalization of inactivity or passivity, now impresses no one. It ceases to impress George; for it is clear now that its ability to move, indeed its very meaning, depends on a carefully adjusted and controlled audience. Violence, repressed for thirty years, boils out of George, as though the buried child in him were raised suddenly and demoniacally by the devilish ritual of Martha and Nick. Howling "YOU SATANIC BITCH!" George leaps at Martha's throat. At one stroke he acquires the will and the ability to retaliate in terms the enemy can understand. For the first time George acts with something like authority, and the others respond with something like respect.

Now George, flexing his physical and his mental muscles, moves to the attack on both levels of the play—the intellectual, involving Nick—and the personal or emotional, involving Martha. On both levels he turns his knowledge into a sharp, heavy weapon with which he may hack at the arrogant masks of power and authority assumed by Nick and Martha.

He turns first on Nick, who discovers that it is possible to see his life and values as less than exemplary. George's story of the little boy was a heavily veiled metaphor of his own shortcomings; but now George tells a second story, and this one proves to be a thinly veiled exposure of Nick and Honey, of the lies and evasions they would like to sweep under the carpet. Honey's father, George points out, was an evangelist who "ran a sort of traveling clip joint" and who amassed a considerable fortune; the fortune sweetened Nick's cup when a hysterical pregnancy trapped him into marriage with Honey. Earlier in the play Nick and George had laughed together over these confidences, just as they had communed over George's tale of the little boy. But George, rinsed of his fears and compassions, now intends to use every weapon at his command, even to the extent of revealing confidences. In striking at Nick with the lowest possible blows, he strikes at what Nick represents— the "pragmatic extension of the big dream"—and makes "history" less inevitable. As Honey rushes out in tears, to be followed by Nick, George shrugs: "the patterns of history." As an intellectual, then, George has assumed an active responsibility for those patterns, for the shape of the present and the shape of the future.

Nick is comparatively easy to dispose of. Martha is something else again. I have already suggested the degree to which Martha and George feed each other's illusions in their curious substitution for love, so that any attempt to destroy a Martha-vision involves a painful George-sacrifice. Between them George and Martha have concocted a make-believe child, an invisible companion, who is as important to George as he is to Martha. Their little "bean bag," as George calls it, gets tossed back and forth, being employed both as a weapon by which they may express their disgust with each other and a shield behind which they may hide their illusions about themselves. "George makes everybody sick," Martha tells her guests. "When our son was just a little boy, he used to . . . throw up all the time, because of George. . . ." Repelled and humiliated, George pleads with her to stop, but Martha, lost in the land of hubris, continues her attack:

> Martha: It got so bad that whenever George came into the room he'd start right in retching, and. . . .

At this point George is lured into the fantasy:

> George: . . . the real reason (*Spits out the words*) our son . . . used to throw up all the time, wife and lover, was nothing more complicated than that he couldn't stand you fiddling at him all the time, breaking into his bedroom with your kimono flying, fiddling at him all the time,. . . .

George's exaggerated disgust with Martha's sexuality (she isn't that sexual) is matched by Martha's exaggerated scorn of George's weakness (he isn't that weak—as Martha herself asserts). Rebounding from his disgust, George describes himself as the wise tutor and guide to whom their son turned "for advice, for information, for love that wasn't mixed with sickness. . . ." Nick reveals how unlikely this description is when George tries to give him "some good advice." To Nick, George is thoroughly ineffectual, a pallid excuse for a man, and he refuses to listen: "You just tend to your knitting, grandma. . . . I'll be O. K." As for Martha, she rather pathetically sees herself as a model mother forced to employ her "greater strength" to save the child from George's weakness. It is unlikely that Martha's

unstable braying would be mistaken for "greater strength." Both defense and attack, then, are rather wide of the mark; the purpose of
the intricate structure that is their make-believe son is to evade
themselves, to evade reality.

But George remembers what Martha forgets: that their son
exists only by agreement, and that it cannot long survive the scru-
tiny of "other people." When he warns Martha in Act I not to "start
in on the bit about the kid"—not to bring their make-believe child
into the party conversation—he is as concerned with the fantasy's
survival as he is with whatever humiliation he might have to endure.
When Martha does speak of their son in Act II, George asserts that
he would rather not talk about it: "I never want to talk about it."
Martha quite correctly points out, "Yes, you do," and George just as
correctly notes, "When we're alone, maybe." And when in Act
III, the new George goads the old Martha into a recitation of
"Our Son," he employs Nick and Honey as a destructive chorus of
"other people."

Inevitably, Martha guesses that something is wrong, or at least
different. In a fairly significant scene she employs tears, pleas, tenderness to bring an end to the new "game." Presumably these devices have worked in the past. But now George refuses to be put off;
he will be kind in his cruelty, rather than cruel in his kindness. After drawing Martha out on the subject of the child—that is, "creating" the child in front of Nick and Honey—George announces to
Martha that their son is dead. It is his way of saying that he, George,
refuses to participate any longer in the monstrous illusions by which
he and Martha have lived. Without his participation the make-
believe child, as well as the illusions embodied in the child, ceases
to exist. Martha understands; she quivers with rage and loss: "NO!
NO! YOU CANNOT DO THAT! YOU CAN'T DECIDE THAT
FOR YOURSELF! I WILL NOT LET YOU DO THAT!" That is
precisely what the new George, the George of will as well as mind,
feels he has the right to do, and feels he must do: "I have the right,
Martha. We never spoke of it; that's all. I could kill him any time
I wanted to."

In killing the child, so enmeshed in the lives of the "parents,"
George effectively kills the old George and Martha. That, I think, is
the point of the rather grim parallelism that Albee contrives: according to George, the make-believe boy died when, "on a country
road, with his learner's permit in his pocket, he swerved, to avoid a
porcupine, and drove straight into a [tree] . . . "; that is the way

the boy of George's novel, described in Act II, smashed his car and killed his father; as the physical father died in Act II, so now the illusory father dies, as well as the illusory mother. It is now possible for George and Martha to be reborn into the reality that is this, not the after life, a life that has never been possessed by either of them. And that no doubt is the point of the requiem mass George recites in Act III. It is not a mass for the repose of a son who never existed, but for the new souls of the living. Light may now strike their perturbed spirits:

> Martha: You didn't have to have him die, George.
> George: *Requiem aeternam dona eis, Domine.*
> Honey: *Et lux perpetua luceat eis.*
> Martha: That wasn't . . . needed. (*A long silence*)
> George: (*Softly*) It will be dawn soon. I think the party's over.

Beyond this, Albee does not carry the play. George is 45 when he puts away childish toys and stops playing childish games. "It will be better," he tells Martha, ". . . maybe." After the one-two punch delivered to Nick and to Martha, new possibilities are open to George on both the intellectual and the social level, but they remain possibilities. Besides, it would scarcely be in keeping with Albee's vision of the world to suggest a behavioral revolution already taking place.

The outline I have just provided is, perhaps, too neat for my own peace of mind. After all, I began by suggesting that the play is rather murky and puzzling. Nor can I pretend that there is any confusion in the overall structure of the play. It is, if anything, too tidy. In all three acts, entitled "Fun and Games," "Walpurgisnacht," and "Exorcism," the same themes and motifs are repeated, though carefully modulated and modified. In "Fun and Games" George sings "Who's Afraid of Virginia Woolf" in an attempt to drown out Martha; in "Walpurgisnacht," the record player blares to the dancing of Martha and Nick—symbolic witch and warlock; in "Exorcism," George chants the requiem. Themes drop into the circular pattern of the play, are submerged, reappear in a new emotional context, drop away, and again slip to the surface. With each turn of the wheel, themes and ideas are developed and redefined.

Nevertheless, there is only slight agreement on the significance and development of the play. The confusion does not seem to be the result of any complexity or depth of idea. Rather, it seems to lie in several innate defects of the play itself. First of all, the two areas of meaning I have pointed to—the emotional and the intellectual—are often separated from each other as the play unfolds. We rarely have individual scenes that make themselves felt on several levels or in several areas of meaning. In one scene George exhibits his intellectual impotence when he toys ironically with Nick on the subject of historical process, actually a matter of serious concern to George. In another scene he reveals his domestic impotence when he writhes at Martha's furious assault on him. While we may relate these scenes to each other conceptually, they are unrelated dramatically. On stage, these scenes do not comment on or develop each other, and the result is a considerable loss of cumulative effect, and a descent into diffuseness and uncertainty.

Second, Albee is trying, I think, to reveal his perceptions in the give-and-take of flat, ordinary conversation. Pointlessly, Martha demands to know the name of a motion picture starring Betty Davis; pointlessly, she and George ramble on for some minutes about it. George's exasperated "I can't remember all the pictures that . . ." is echoed by Martha's insistence that she can't remember the name of one of the male actors: "I can't remember his name, for God's sake. What's the name of the *picture*? I want to know what the name of the *picture* is." After Martha announces that she has invited a new faculty couple to drop over at two o'clock in the morning, a similar, equally senseless, dialogue evolves:

> George: Good Lord, Martha . . . do you know what time
> it . . . *Who's* coming over?
> Martha: What's-their-name.
> George: Who?
> Martha: WHAT'S-THEIR-NAME!
> George: Who what's-their-name?
> Martha: I don't know what their name is, George. . . .
> you met them tonight . . . they're new . . . he's in the
> math department, or something. . . .

Albee apparently intends such dialogue to carry a good deal of meaning. The attempt is itself intriguing, and dramatically courageous, but since Albee fails to provide a clear enough framework for the play, a framework that would enable us to interpret the ordinary in an extraordinary way, the result again is vagueness and diffuseness.

Third, there is an unfortunate imbalance in the play. The remarkably effective scenes in which Martha humiliates George time after time drown the rest of the action; the pattern of ideas I have described never really functions dramatically. Yet the significance of the entire last act depends upon an awareness of this pattern. Albee attempts to kick the act to its feet with the ceremonial death of the make-believe child, but the symbol never really works. From *Zoo Story* on, Albee has been obsessed with the image of the orphaned or alienated child, and he ascribes to it considerably more weight and power than it necessarily has. And that is no doubt true of some of the other scenes and symbols.

But whatever else one may say about it, the play is both moving and powerful. It remains a dramatic experience that cannot be chop-logiced out of existence. To say that Albee's later plays have not measured up to *Who's Afraid* is not saying very much, for *Who's Afraid* establishes an extraordinarily high level.

The Novelist as Playwright:
Baldwin, McCullers, and Bellow

by Louis Phillips

There may have been a time when a man could label himself simply as a writer and be secure of his role in society. But such days, if they ever existed at all, have long since vanished, for in our present age of specialization, the term *writer* is far too vague. We want to know exactly what he writes, in what form is he particularly adept. Is he a novelist or a playwright or a poet or an essayist? If he is an essayist, what kind of an essayist, formal or informal? What kind of a novelist, serious or popular (pretending to ourselves that they are mutually exclusive categories)?

It is somewhat of a paradox that in a time of immense diversity we do not expect our artists to be diverse, for we have learned or are in the process of learning, from such men as Marshal McCluhan, that each medium of expression is a message in itself and that it requires a life-time of study to know how one form or one medium controls and modifies the content that we put into it. Thus, when leading novelists turn to the theatre, we are inclined to give their creations in the new medium only cursory attention. We say to ourselves, "Well now I see that Bellow is trying his hand at the theatre. I hope he gets over the bug soon and gets back to his serious work, back to the novel where he belongs," ignoring the fact that novelists often turn playwrights (or

145

vice versa) not out of choice but out of necessity. What they want to say, have to say, cannot be expressed in any other way. Of course, novelists can be attracted to the theatre for many other reasons as well: the lure of money (although the present financial state of serious theatre on and off-Broadway makes this possibility highly unlikely); the desire to prove ones' versatility, or, perhaps, even to escape the solitude that forms the brunt of a writer's daily existence. This last possibility is one that Miss Carson McCullers has advanced in her preface to the published version of her play, *The Square Root of Wonderful*:

> Many novelists have been attracted to the theatre—Fitzgerald, Wolfe, James, and Joyce. Perhaps this is because of the loneliness of a writer's life—the unaccustomed joy of participating creatively with others is marvelous to a writer. It is rare that a writer is equally skilled as a novelist and a playwright.

It is indeed rare that a writer be equally skilled as a playwright and as a novelist. James Baldwin, Carson McCullers, and Saul Bellow, to name just three contemporary novelists who have turned their talents to the theatre, are perhaps, all three, better novelists than they are playwrights, but such an evaluation may be quite useless in the long-run. The important fact is that they have all felt the need to use the dramatic form to express, develop, and amplify the themes that have formed the basis of their many novels. Carson McCullers' most successful play, in fact, *The Member of the Wedding* was originally a novel, and her *The Ballad of the Sad Cafe* has been adapted to the stage by Edward Albee. Even a novelist as highly skeptical of the worth of the American theatre as is James Baldwin once adapted his novel, *Giovanni's Room* for an Actors Studio workshop presentation.

I. JAMES BALDWIN

Of the three novelist/playwrights under discussion, James Baldwin appears to be the one least entranced by the American theatre, for he has written that he does not possess "much respect for what goes on in the American Theatre" and that it seems to him "a series, merely, of commercial speculations, stale, repetitious, and timid." But, in spite of his protestations, Baldwin has been attracted to the dramatic form. His first play, *The Amen Corner*, was produced at Harvard University; his second was his adaptation of *Giovanni's Room;* and his third, and best-known play, is the full-length *Blues For Mister Charlie.*

It will be surprising to no one familiar with James Baldwin's novels and essays that his play *Blues For Mister Charlie* is concerned with racial inequality and injustice, and that it is based, in part, on the shooting of Emmett Till, the young Negro who was murdered for whistling at a white woman. What is amazing though is Baldwin's ability to see the white community of a small southern town through its own eyes and his ability to portray the wider issues involved in a racial murder: the terrible self-deceptions that racial murderers must live by. Baldwin, in his notes to the play, has stated:

> What is ghastly and really almost hopeless in our racial situation now is that the crimes we have committed are so great and so unspeakable that the acceptance of this knowledge would lead, literally, to madness. The human being, then, in order to protect himself, closes his eyes, compulsively repeats his crimes, and enters a spiritual darkness which no one can describe.

In *Blues* ("Mister Charlie" is a slang term referring to all white men) Lyle Britten is a white store-owner who murders the son of a Negro minister, but who refuses to recognize that he has committed any crime. In Lyle's eyes the events that brought about the boy's death are quite simple: the boy was a dope-addict from New York City and had insulted Lyle's wife. All that Lyle wanted from the boy was an apology, but when the boy refused, Lyle had no choice but to kill him.

> LYLE: I had to kill him then. I'm a white man! Can't nobody talk that way to *me!* I had to go and get my pickup truck and load him in it—I had to carry him on my back—and carry him out to the high weeds. And I dumped him in the weeds, face down. And then I come on home to my good Jo here.
>
> JO: Come on, Lyle. We got to get on home. We got to get the little one home now.
>
> LYLE: And I ain't sorry. I want you to know that I ain't sorry.

Although Lyle has the murder of two Negroes to his "credit,"
he firmly believes that he has nothing against the black race.
He tells his good friend, Parnell James, the editor of a local
newspaper,

> You sound like you think I got something against colored
> folks—but I don't. I never have, not in all my life.
> But I'll be damned if I'll mix with them. That's *all*. I
> don't want no big buck nigger lying up next to Josephine
> and that's where all this will lead to and you know it as
> as well as I do! I'm against it and I'll do anything I have
> to do to stop it, yes, I will.

In his own eyes, Lyle is acting in the name of righteousness, not
prejudice, and the terrifying irony is that he truly believes that
he has nothing against colored folks. Lyle has many virtues: he is
hard-working; he loves his wife and his son; and he is good to his
friends and his friends are loyal to him. At the same time, however,
Lyle carries around inside of him an indescribable blindness, a
double-standard too vile to recognize. He says that he'll be damned
if he will mix with colored folks, pretends to himself that they are
a race apart, and yet he freely goes to bed with Negro women.
"Poon Tang" is what he likes, and, in fact, before the events re-
counted in the play, Lyle has shot one man—the husband of a
Negro woman Lyle had taken a fancy to. But, in his own mind,
Lyle is unable to allow a Negro man to sleep with a white woman.
As Richard Henry, the boy murdered by Lyle, puts it, white men
"can rape and kill our women and we can't do nothing. But if
we touch one of their dried-up, pale-assed women, we get our
nuts cut off."

In retaliation to the attitude of men like Lyle, young Richard
enjoys messing up the lives of white girls he has known in New
York. Richard tells Juanita, his Negro girl-friend, that he wants to
screw up the minds of his white-women forever and that he wants
them to be sad for knowing him. Revenge is the underlying
motivation for all of Richard's actions. He wants revenge for the
injustice against his people, and he wants to revenge the death
of his mother, who was pushed down the steps of a white-hotel.
To the eyes of the white community, Richard is an out-sider from
the North, a dope-addict trying to kick the habit, an insolent and
arrogant nigger who fools around with white women. Thus, in his
play, Baldwin pulls no punches. Instead of portraying a meek and

innocent Negro up against a Simon Legree, Baldwin presents the problem as it is seen by a small Southern White Community. How often have we heard it said that a certain Negro would not have been shot if he had stayed up North where he belonged and had not come into the South, looking for trouble? It is most likely the same argument advanced by the white man who wounded James Meredith on his famous march. But, in *Blues*, Baldwin reverses our expectations and the more we root for Lyle Britten, the more successful the play becomes. Poor Lyle—all he wants is a simple apology from a Negro who has deliberately insulted his wife, and the boy won't give in. Knowing what we do about Lyle's upbringing, his beliefs, and his environment, we know that Lyle has no choice but to kill the boy—we know it. As sure as the sun rises and the sun sets, we know that Richard Henry is going to be killed, and we say to ourselves, "Why doesn't that boy apologize? Why doesn't he use his head? Why is he being so stupid?" But the true villain of the play is not Lyle Britten, nor is it Richard Henry. Baldwin knows that Lyle is every bit the victim Richard Henry is, and that the crime depicted is our crime, that we are the ones who have created men like Lyle Britten. In Baldwin's eyes, ". . . we, the American people, have created him, he is our servant; it is we who put the cattle-prodder in his hands, and we are responsible for the crimes he commits."

Baldwin points out in his notes that *Blues For Mr. Charlie* takes place in Plaguetown, U.S.A., and that "The plague is race, the plague is our concept of Christianity: and this raging plague has the power to destroy every human relationship." It may seem strange that Baldwin sees Christianity as a plague, but religion's failure to sustain and to liberalize the visions of the characters in the play is one of the play's major themes. In the white community of Plaguetown, Christianity is represented by Reverend Phelps, a reverend who sees the blacks as a race misled by communists and rabble-rousers:

> REVEREND PHELPS: Their minds have been turned.
> They have turned away from God. They're a simple
> people—warm hearted and good-natured. But they
> are very easily led, and now they are harkening to
> the counsel of these degenerate Communist race-
> mixers. And they don't know what terrible harm
> they can bring on themselves—and on us all.

But Negroes such as Richard Henry and his friends are neither warm-hearted or simple, and they have very little reason to be so. Hence, they are far beyond Reverend Phelps' comprehension. Phelps has been raised in the same community, same environment, and exposed to the same system of beliefs that Lyle Britten has, so it is quite natural that men like Phelps cannot emerge as the true leaders in a time of crisis. When the Christian leaders of the South should have been breaking down the doors of prejudice, they, instead, have reiterated the stock-phrases and blind-values of their community, or they have remained silent. But, if Christianity has failed the white community, Baldwin wants us to know that it has failed the Negro community as well. Far too often, men like Minister Meridian Henry, father of the slain boy, turn to Christianity because it is the only institution which allows the Negro any shred of dignity. Minister Henry himself questions his Christian dedication when he tells Parnell,

> . . . I've been thinking, I've had to think—would I have
> *been* such a Christian if I hadn't been born black? Maybe
> I *had* to become a Christian in order to have any dignity
> at all. Since I wasn't a man in men's eyes, then I could
> be a man in the eyes of God. . . .

After his son is murdered, Minister Henry struggles valiantly against the failure of his religion, and he speaks out against all the darkness within him, the spiritual darkness in all people, black and white: "This darkness rules us, and grows, in black and white alike. I have set my face against the darkness, I will not let it conquer me." In the final scenes of the play, however, during the trial, darkness overcomes the entire community, and Lyle Britten's trial becomes a shambles of lies.

On the stand, and under oath, Minister Henry claims that his son had never carried a gun:

> THE STATE: You never saw him with a gun? Or with
>   any other weapon?
> MERIDIAN: No.
> THE STATE: Reverend Henry—are you in a position to
>   swear your son never carried arms?
> MERIDIAN: Yes. I can swear to it. The only time
>   the subject was ever mentioned he told me that he

was stronger than white people and could live without a gun.

In fact, Richard had given his father a gun to hold for safe-keeping.
Mother Henry, Richard's grandmother, had also seen the gun, but
she too denies the weapon's existence.

> MOTHER HENRY: I don't know where you got that
> story, or why you keep harping on it. I never saw
> no gun.

In order to prevent Lyle from being found guilty, the white wit-
nesses also distort the facts. Although Richard Henry had not as-
saulted Lyle's wife physically, Lyle's wife claims that the boy had
attempted to rape her. Also, much of the trial hinges on whether
or not Richard had possessed pornographic snapshots of white
women, pictures that have nothing to do with Lyle's guilt, but
which have their effect upon the emotions of the jury. In order
to protect his race, each individual deceives himself and others, each
one rationalizing his deceit by silently appealing to a concept of
racial justice or to Christianity, for the responsibility for what has
happened is so overwhelming that it would lead, as Baldwin states,
literally to madness.

In *Blues* the man caught in the middle of the conflict is
Parnell James, for he is a friend of both Meridian Henry and Lyle
Britten, and, as such, he really has no place in the town. His
liberalism shows, perhaps, what attitudes the citizens of the town
should grow towards, but his views are more tolerated than admired,
more puzzling to the townspeople than tolerated. The majority of
people in the town do not know Parnell's position on important
issues because they refuse to read his "communist" newspaper. The
Reverend Phelps even tells Parnell, ". . . we didn't really mind your
attitude, and your paper didn't matter to us, we never read it
anyway." Parnell's major failure in the eyes of the white community,
however, is that his attitudes are not the same as the ones possessed by his parents. Lyle Britten can be admired because Lyle
has followed in his father's footsteps, and one of the townspeople
comments,

> ELLIS: Lyle's just like his daddy. You can't beat him.
> The harder a thing is, well, the surer you can be that
> old Old Lyle Britten will do it.

But Parnell is not like Lyle, nor like Lyle's parents, nor even like his own parents. In this respect, his presence in the white community parallels that of Richard's presence in the Negro community. Both are, in one way or another, outsiders, and both represent a sharp break with the traditions that engulf them. Both are deeply concerned with the problem of social justice, and to Parnell social justice means

> . . . that if I have a hundred dollars, and I'm black, and you have a hundred dollars, and you're white, I should be able to get as much value for *my* hundred dollars—my black hundred dollars—as you get for your *white* hundred dollars. It also means that I should have an equal opportunity to *earn* that hundred dollars—

During Lyle's trial, Parnell tries to serve the facts as well as his friendship for both Meridian and Lyle, and his testimony reveals that he cannot take sides in favor of one friendship over another. Thus, he becomes a solitary figure in the community, his position partially symbolized by the answer Richard's girl-friend gives Parnell at the play's end:

> PARNELL: Can I join you in the march, Juanita? Can I walk with you?
> JUANITA: Well, we can walk in the same direction.

At the conclusion of another play about a small southern town, *Inherit the Wind,* the lawyer Drummond picks up the *Bible* and Darwin's *Origin of Species* and holds them together in his hands. At the conclusion of *Blues for Mister Charlie,* Minister Meridian Henry places the *Bible* with Richard Henry's gun.

> MERIDIAN: You know, for us, it all began with the Bible and the gun. Maybe it will end with the Bible and the gun.
> JUANITA: What did you do with the gun, Meridian?
> PARNELL: You have the gun—Richard's gun?
> MERIDIAN: Yes. In the pulpit. Under the Bible. Like the pilgrims of old.

Like Lyle, Preacher Henry is speaking in the name of righteousness, not prejudice, but his belief that the Bible and the gun go hand in hand is just one more lie that he will have to close his eyes to, another lie for us to close our eyes to.

II. CARSON McCULLERS

If James Baldwin's play dissects an entire community or social evil, Carson McCullers' territory of concern is far more intimate and closely-knit for her two full length plays, *The Member of the Wedding* and *The Square Root of Wonderful* center around the family unit and focus upon the problems of one or two members within each unit. Encouraged by Tennessee Williams to adapt her novel, *The Member of the Wedding,* to the stage, Miss McCullers centered her first play around an adolescent girl named Frankie Addams and the frustrations resulting from Frankie's inability to be either an adult or a child. Frankie's awkward transition from childhood to womanhood leaves her with a bewildering aloneness, and when we first meet Frankie she has been turned down as a prospective member of a girl's club. The girls refuse to accept Frankie into their club because she is too young. Berenice, the family maid, tries to comfort Frankie and encourages her to form a club of her own:

> BERENICE: Frankie, the whole idea of a club is that
> there are members who are included and the non-
> members who are not included. Now what you ought
> to do is to round up a club of your own.
> And you could be president yourself.
> (*There is a pause.*)
> FRANKIE: Who could I get?
> BERENICE: Why, those little children you hear playing
> in the neighborhood.

But Frankie doesn't want to be president of a gang of little kids. She has out-grown them. At the same time, however, the adults won't permit her to belong to any of their "clubs." Berenice was married at the age of thirteen, but, at the same age, Frankie hasn't even been out on a date. Even Charles, Frankie's pet alley cat, deserts her and goes off to look for a "lady-friend." In her loneliness, she takes out her frustrations by teasing her friend, John Henry, the white boy from next door, and she wails disconsolately, "Maybe I'd be better off in jail." Later she says to herself, "Seems like everybody goes off and leaves me." One of the persons who is going off and leaving Frankie is her brother Jarvis, for Jarvis is getting married. Thus, when Frankie is included as a member of the wedding, it becomes the single most important event in her life. She decides that after the ceremony she will travel around the world with her brother and his wife. She will then belong, not only to Jarvis and Janice, but to the whole world as well:

> FRANKIE: . . . We will have thousands and thousands of friends. And we will belong to so many clubs that we can't keep track of all of them. We will be members of the whole world. Boyoman! Manoboy!

But her dreams are short-lived, when she is dragged crying from the wedding-car.

> JOHN HENRY: They put Frankie out of the wedding. They hauled her out of the wedding car.
> BERENICE: Don't tease your cousin, John Henry.
> FRANKIE: It was a frame-up all around.

Paralleling Frankie's "frame-up" and her emotional isolation is the backdrop of the Negro community in the play. Honey Camden Brown, Berenice's fifth husband, is a "worthless nigger" in the eyes of Frankie's father, and Honey can find no way to make his presence felt but by threatening white-men with razors or through smoking reefers or by getting drunk. Like Frankie, Honey and his friends can't belong to any "clubs" either and they must take out their humiliation on other people. Berenice tells him

> You troubled and beat down and try to take it out on a little boy. You and Frankie just alike. The club girls don't elect her and she turns on John Henry too. When folks are lonesome and left out, they turn so mean.

Both Frankie and Honey want to say "we" instead of "I." Frankie admits

> The trouble with me is that for a long time I have been just an "I" person. All other people can say "We." When Bernice says "we" she means her lodge and church and colored people. Soldiers can say "we" and mean the army. All people belong to a "we" except me.

There is a delicate irony involved in Frankie's speech, for she looks to Berenice as a perfect example of "we" but, at the end of the play, it is Berenice who becomes the most isolated. Her husband hangs himself in jail when he is caught for pulling a razor on a white-man; John Henry, whom Berenice calls "her little boy," dies of meningitis; and, when Frankie's father decides to move into a new house, Berenice gives notice and refuses to go with them. Frankie, on the other hand, makes friends with a new girl in the neighborhood, Mary Littlejohn, a friendship that signals Frankie's acceptance into a new and wider world. Where Berenice was a member, she no longer belongs; where Frankie was an outcast, she now becomes a full-fledged member.

If there is any relation at all between Carson McCullers' first play and her second, *The Square Root of Wonderful*, it is perhaps summed up in Berenice's statement, "When folks are lonesome and left out, they turn so mean." It may well be the unifying theme throughout all of Miss McCullers' writing, for her second play takes its title from the reversal of an idea set forth by one of its characters—"the sin of hurting people's feelings. Of humiliating a person. That is the square root of sin. It's the same as murder."

Drawing upon the memory of her husband's failure to become a successful writer and upon memories of her mother, Miss McCullers attempts to create a tragic-comedy around the decision of Mollie Lovejoy, a woman who must decide whether to remarry her ex-husband Phillip for the third time or to marry John Tucker, an architect who is living in the Lovejoy house as a boarder. When the play opens, Phillip is divorced from Molly and has been in a sanitorium, following an attempt at suicide. His re-entrance into the household, though, is signalled by his son's nightmare in the opening moments of Act One:

> PARIS: I dreamed a burglar was in the house. A dark
> man in a kind of burglar's cap—at first I didn't see
> his face.

Paris identifies the burglar with his father, and, in fact, Phillip is a kind of burglar. He sneaks into the Lovejoy house in the hope of stealing back his wife and his teen-age son. Although Mollie is still sexually attracted to her ex-husband, they both know that their love has undergone great changes. Phillip freely admits to Molly that he has not returned for love:

> MOLLIE: If you don't love me, why did you come
> back?
> PHILLIP: Like the sick person watches the well. Like
> the dying watches the living. No, Mollie, it's not
> love.

MOLLIE: Then what is it?

PHILLIP: Without you I am exposed, I am skinless.
From the beginning you knew I had to live in a co-
coon. You knew I had to live with you and be pro-
tected. It is not my fault, it is just an act of nature.

Phillip would use his weakness to win Mollie back, and when
he discovers that the architect wants to marry her, he attempts to
humiliate his rival.

JOHN: Don't mind me. Don't mind me.

PHILLIP: I'm not minding you. You come before me
like a gnat.

MOLLIE: John was a champion boxer in high school.

PHILLIP: Oh, a tough guy—in high school.

MOLLIE: John was in the navy for four years.

PHILLIP: And a hero, too.

It is Mollie who must put up a valiant effort to keep both
men from being humiliated—the square root of sin—for both men
have experienced failure in their chosen professions. As an architect,
John is a failure in his inability to achieve any recognition and
admits that his life has "No back or front or depth. No design or
meaning." Phillip is a failure because he has been unable to live
up to his initial success as a novelist. His sense of humiliation and
failure finally becomes so deep that, when he fails in his attempt
to recapture Mollie, he commits suicide by driving his car off the
road and into a pond.

As a play, *The Square Root of Wonderful* has not been nearly
so successful or admired as *The Member of the Wedding*. Part
of *Square Root's* failure might be traced to an obvious indebtedness
to Tennessee Williams' *The Glass Menagerie*. The remainder of the
Lovejoy family—Phillip's sister, Loreena, and his mother—appear to
be Laura and Amanda Wingfield in a slightly different setting.
Mother Lovejoy's speech to Loreena about sex and about the good-
old-days reads as if it were right out of the Williams' play.

MOTHER LOVEJOY: . . . in my day a girl didn't have
to depend on that three-letter word. Those were the
days when charm, beauty, and vivaciousness were
appreciated. Just simple allure was enough. Gentle-
men came from as far as Chattahooche County and
Joplin to court me. I was sought after, admired,
proposed to, feted. I was the belle of Society City.

Like Amanda Wingfield, Mother Lovejoy was abandoned by her
husband and left with two children and little funds. Like Laura,
Loreena is well on her way to becoming an old-maid, for she is
shy, diffident, and experiences romance only in her day-dreams.
Mother Lovejoy is always pushing Loreena toward possible hus-
band/victims.

Another possible reason for the play's lack of success may be
found in an essential difference between the novel and the play.
Carson McCullers herself has written

> I was aware of the risk in alternating comic and tragic
> scenes, aware that it confuses the same audience who can
> respond readily to a single situation with both laughter and
> tears. This is mostly true in the theatre; a reader of novels
> is more emotionally flexible because he has time to reflect
> before he is pushed on to the next action.

It may well be that the tragic-comic form is more suitable to the
novel than it is to the theatre.

III. SAUL BELLOW

In an article reviewing movies for the magazine *Horizon* (January, 1963), Saul Bellow took the "mass-produced insights" of the
motion-picture industry. He wrote

> 'Insight,' a proud word for things that millions of people
> have learned by rote, stands now in the very center of the
> entertainment industry. Often the plot and all actions of a
> movie are derived from a nucleus of psychological illumi-
> nation. Heroes are those who struggle heroically with neu-
> roses, while villains are afflicted with sadistic or sadomaso-
> chistic difficulties that we are invited to understand sym-
> pathetically, with Hollywood insight.

Bellow's conclusion was that the excitement produced by Hollywood's
psychological morality (if there is any such animal) "gives us the
illusion that we are thinking seriously about life."

Although it is often quite unfair to use a man's own words
against himself, it appears that Bellow's appraisal of Hollywood
movies might well apply to Bellow's own novels, to *Herzog* especially, and to his full-length play, *The Last Analysis.* It cannot be

denied that Bellow is an important novelist, and yet, the characters
he creates, from Joseph in *The Dangling Man,* to Moses Herzog,
to Bummidge in *The Last Analysis,* are characters who are trapped
in the illusion that they are thinking seriously about life. Also,
his novels and his play are constructed in such a manner that the
reader or viewer is not able to break through the confines of that
illusion. If Bellow were a true satirist, his position as a novelist
would be staggering to consider, but melodrama and satire do not
make very good bedfellows, and Bellow's characters have a flair
for the melodramatic and the desperate tone of pathos, where both
the flair and the tone do great damage to the satirical intent.

In *The Last Analysis,* Bummidge, like Herzog, gathers his
strength from blatant self-examination, from the illusion that he is
thinking seriously about himself. Briefly stated, the plot of the
play concerns a closed-circuit telecast of the psychological life of
a has-been comedian named Bummidge. The telecast, improvised by
and paid for by the comedian, is to be beamed to the American
Psychiatrist Association, and Bummy's lawyer, friends, relatives,
mistress, and ex-wife gather in the loft of a warehouse on New
York's West Side to take part in the unique experiment, to act out
various events in Bummy's past. The first act of the play shows the
telecast in preparation: Bummy's financial needs; his arguments
with his son, Max; and his acting out with his sister of the time when
Bummy was eleven years old, when she caught him in her room, fond-
ling her underthings. To get his sister to re-enact the episode,
Bummy pleads to her on his knees:

> I'm on an expedition to recover the forgotten truth. Madge,
> you have no idea what human beings really are: the stages
> of psyche—polymorphous, oral, anal, narcisstic. It's fantas-
> tic, intricate, complicated, hidden. How can you live with-
> out knowing? Madge, look deep! Infinite and deep!

In Bummy's view, he is indeed on the expedition to discover
the truth, and the scond act of the play is the actual telecast
to the gathering of psychiatrists, and to a select group of comedians
and television magnates; the program's rambling failures; and its
ultimate acceptance by a major television network who wishes to
use it as a regular series. On this level, the playwright appears
to be spoofing Freudian psychology and the peculiar insanities and
inanities of much popular entertainment. In short, the play is a
dramatic version of the ideas set forth in Bellow's movie review for

Horizon, a thrust against manufactured insight. Bellow, however, has written, in an author's note to the published version of the play, that his play is

> . . . not simply a spoof of Freudian psychology, though certain analysts have touchily interpreted it as such. Its real subject is the mind's comical struggle for survival in an environment of Ideas—its fascination with metaphors, and the peculiarly literal and solemn manner in which Americans dedicate themselves to programs, fancies or brainstorms.

The first production of the play, starring Sam Levine as Bummidge, had only a short run on broadway, and Bellow attributes the play's failure, in part, to the neglect of the *mental* comedy. In the published version of *The Last Analysis,* he has attempted to restore the missing ingredient, but as one reads the play, the comedy still seems to be lacking. Is it that *mental* comedy is in itself incapable of being expressed on stage through physical actions, that we must use metaphor to ridicule metaphor? All comedy is mental on the part of the spectator because it requires us to assume a particular attitude toward a given set of circumstances, but Bellow's emphasis is clearly not on the spectator's mental comedy, but on the comedy that takes place in the mind of his main character. Bummidge is a television clown who wishes to be an intellectual. Like Herzog, Bummy is well-read, so much so that Winkleman, Bummy's lawyer, calls him "a junkie on thought." In Winkleman's opinion,

> Earnestness has been the ruin of my cousin. High-mindedness. The suckers had their mouths open for yucks —he fed them Aristotle, Kierkegaard, Freud. Who needs another homemade intellectual?

Bummy, however, is not the only one ruined by earnestness; Bellow's spoof is ruined by too much earnestness also. Bummy's intense seriousness creates an aura of pathos that is difficult to penetrate by laughter alone. If Bummy were simply pretending to knowledge in order to advance himself, then his eventual rebirth would provide comic possibilities. The "Intelligent-Quotient" fraud or the arrogant intellectual or the pedant have all been the butts for jokes of our keenest comic-writers. But Bummidge's superficial evaluation of his dreams, his manufactured "insights" (which

Bellow inveighs against in his movie review) are clearly leading to self-destruction, self-destruction that he dearly invites, and self-destruction goes against the comic vein. The fact that Bummidge is mentally ill can be made comic, but it is not comic in itself. In the movie, *What's New, Pussycat?*, itself a spoof of psychiatry, Paula Prentice plays a woman who constantly attempts suicide by taking over-doses of sleeping-pills. Her characterization becomes comic only because the screen-writer, in this case Woody Allen, does not take her destruction seriously, nor do we; we never believe for one moment that she is going to die from her foolish actions. Also, constant repetition of the same action becomes comic by upsetting the laws of chance and our expectations. The difference between Woody Allen's spoof and Saul Bellow's is a difference of earnestness. Bellow is too involved with his characters to satirize them; he cares too much for Bummidge, for Herzog, for Joseph K., and his concern shows through in his tone. Spoofing should be fun, and when it is not, it becomes a form of terror. Bellow, in trying to create a spoof *and* something-else, ends up with a play that is far less than a spoof.

Again, it goes back to the assumption that underlies Bellow's novels and plays—that the mind's struggle for survival in an environment of ideas is a comical one. It is an assumption that is not necessarily so. There is nothing *inherently* comic about the mind's struggle to survive, any more than there is something inherently comic about civilization being destroyed by an ATOM-bomb blast. Such situations, of course, can be made comic, but only if the playwright allows us to set our earnestness aside for awhile. Comedy enables us to release tensions, but in *The Last Analysis,* Bellow constantly increases our tensions, for there are few things on this planet more pathetic than a comedian who is not funny. Bummidge's curtain speech in the final act of the play is as far from the spirit of spoofing as *Herzog* is from the spirit of tragedy.

> . . . I wanted to do it. I did it of my own free will. *Thinking*: Or did those people force freedom on me? Now, where is the butcher's telegram? We have things to do. Work! Work! Onwards to the Trilby. We have to tear up the floors and purge the smell of blood. Go, Imogen, and let in my scientific colleagues. They've been waiting. I will put on my toga. The trilby will be run like Plato's academy. PUTS

ON TOGA, ARRANGES FOLDS. The Bummidge
Institute of nonsense. We deserve a modern sky-
scraper like the United Nations, but the poor, the
sad, the bored and tedious on the earth will trust us
better for beginning so humbly. And we will train
people in the Method and send them as missionaries
to England, to Germany, to all those bleak and sadistic countries. I am so moved! What a struggle I've
had. It took me so long to get through the brutal
stage of life. And when I was through with it, the
mediocre was waiting for me. And now that's done
with, and I am ready for the sublime. HE RAISES
HIS ARMS IN A GREAT GESTURE.

The elements of spoof are present, but Bellow wants us to
focus our attention on something else entirely: the mind's inability
to escape its own concept of mind. In doing so, however, he
works at cross-purposes to himself. At the end of the play, we
know as little about Bummidge's mind as Bummy does himself. We
have been saved from glib, easily manufactured insights, but have
we been offered anything at all? All we know is that Bummy
is greatly confused for we see a great deal of confusion on stage.
But confusion and chaos are only comic when they are organized
through unconfused and unchaotic minds. To express confusion
through confusion is not art; to create boredom on the stage or
on the screen by boring the audience is to misunderstand metaphor.
The *mental* comedy, the ingredient Bellow wishes to emphasize, will
always seem to be missing from his play because we cannot place
the human mind on the stage. We can place human beings on a
stage, men and women who use or disuse their minds, men and
women who try to tell us who they are and what they think
through actions and/or through language, the choice of metaphor.
The human comedy, even Charlie Chaplin swinging his cane and
shuffling off into the sunset, is and always will be mental comedy.
In *The Last Analysis*, Saul Bellow is a satirist defeated by his
own earnestness. He wants us to see clearly the difference between
"thinking that we are thinking seriously about life" and "thinking
seriously about life," but the materials that he uses to show us
the difference, from Herzog's letters to Bummidge's telecast, only
cause us to wonder about what Saul Bellow seriously thinks. Or
has the illusion trapped the illusionist?

FOOTNOTES

1. James Baldwin. "Notes for *Blues*" in *Blues For Mister Charlie* (N.Y. Dial Press, 1964), pp. xiii-xv.

2. Carson McCullers, "Personal Preface" to *The Square Root of Wonderful* (Boston: Houghton Mifflin Company, 1958).

3. Saul Bellow. "Movies: The Mass Produced Insight," *Horizon*, V (January, 1963), pp. 111-113.

4. S. Bellow. "An Author's Note," in *The Last Analysis* (N.Y.: Dial Press, 1964).

Off-Broadway and the
New Realism

by BERNARD F. DUKORE

To many people, the American theatre means Broadway, and Broadway has become associated with neon signs and phony glitter, of the opulence and gaudiness that masks shallowness or emptiness. In short, Broadway means the commercial theatre, and the Broadway theatres are the *boulevard* theatres of New York City, which is the theatrical capital of the United States.

But there is an alternative, off-Broadway. Although most of the off-Broadway theatres are in New York's Greenwich Village or the Lower East Side, off-Broadway is not so much a matter of location as it is state of mind. If Broadway evokes images of shallowness, sugariness, and superfical slickness, then off-Broadway brings to mind the image of the dedicated artist in the loft. If Broadway is commercialdom, then off-Broadway is anti-commercialdom.

However, these contrasts that I have indicated are not rigid compartments; they are generalizations, and—this is the case with all generalizations—exceptions can be found. We should not forget that Broadway has presented plays by Bernard Shaw, Bertolt Brecht, Albert Camus, and Jean-Paul Sartre; nor should we forget that off-Broadway has presented plays by Maxwell Anderson, Agatha Christie, Cole Porter, and Tennessee Williams. When we find stars whose names have great commercial value—such as Shelley Winters, Eli

Wallach, Franchot Tone, and Montgomery Clift—performing off-Broadway, the lines separating the two become blurred.

This does not mean that there are no differences; the general points of contrast still hold. Definitives are based on the center, not in the edges. Usually, off-Broadway produces the *avant-garde* playwrights while Broadway produces the *derriere-garde*. Since the financial failure of *Waiting for Godot* on Broadway, Beckett's New York address has been off-Broadway. By and large, this has been the New York address of Ionesco, Pinter, and Genet as well. Ionesco's *Rhinoceros* was presented on Broadway, but this play is his most conventional and therefore most commercial comedy. Pinter's *The Caretaker* was presented on Broadway, but this was the importation of a London hit, with the London cast intact. Genet has yet to move to "respectable" Broadway. When the *avant-garde* gets to Broadway, it is either an internationally famous play that is thought to have sufficient snob appeal to be successful, a not particularly *avant-garde* play by an *avant-garde* playwright, or an importation of a London success. Also, off-Broadway is more congenial to the one-act play. A bill of one-act plays on Broadway is a rare occasion; such programs are considered to be death at the box office. Off-Broadway, production costs are lower. Producers are more willing to take risks. This may account in part for the production of European *avant-garde* playwrights off-Broadway: these dramatists often tend to write short rather than long plays. Off-Broadway, too, is the home of the revival: Euripides, Aristophanes, Marlowe, Ford, Chekhov, Ibsen, Pirandello. When there is a revival on Broadway, it is either an import from England or a star vehicle or both.

But are there native off-Broadway playwrights? Do they form a "school" or at least a trend? Although it sometimes seems that the only "school" they represent is that of American individualism, with each dramatist firmly determined to be as unlike any of his fellows as he possibly can, nevertheless several clusters may be seen.

There are, to begin with, the traditional playwrights. William Henley's one-act play, *Mrs. Dally has a Lover,* is a sensitive story of a thirty-eight-year-old married woman and her eighteen-year-old lover; its curtain-raiser, *Whisper Into My Good Ear,* is a tale of two lonely old men in a park—one nearly blind, the other homosexual—who find friendship on the brink of death. Murray Schisgal's *The Typist* presents a male and a female typist growing older in one uninterrupted act and is a vehicle for two star actors; its curtain-raiser, *The Tiger,* is a comic yarn about a sex-starved abductor whose victim finds him sufficiently interesting to have, on her own volition, an affair with him. All four of these plays are competent, craftsmanlike pieces of work by playwrights of professional calibre. But they are not at all different from the usual Broadway product—except for the fact that they are one-act plays. Hence, I suspect, their production off-Broadway. Jack Richardson's *The Prodigal* is a retelling of the *Oresteia* in which circumstances, rather than free will, force Orestes to abandon his intellectual detachment and avenge a father who has been a stranger to him and to espouse a cause he despises. Although *The Prodigal* is a remarkably adult play, its dramaturgy is conventional. However, a "Greek play" by an unknown author is too much of a risk for Broadway; thus, off-Broadway. Then there is Edward Albee, the United States' most praised young playwright. *Zoo Story*, (his first and probably his best play) is a perfectly conventional, realistic, psychological drama. It is also a one-acter, and so it was left to off-Broadway to "discover" him on a double bill with Samuel Beckett. Albee left realism for a while with his obvious and obviously derivative *The American Dream* and *Sandbox*, but he abandoned the non-realistic mode and made his Broadway debut with (I do not think this is coincidential) his first full-length play, the traditionally realistic *Who's Afraid of Virginia Woolf?*

Several of our young playwrights thumb their noses at realism. James Day, for example, in the *The Redemptor*, an Ionesco-like parable about The Bomb—written, I must add, before he had read a word of Ionesco's—spins a story of an ancient scientist named Julius Apocalypse who, with his wife Albatross, lives in a latter-day version of an ivory tower: the thirty-seventh floor of a walk-up tenement in New York City. Apocalypse has invented a bomb which will blow up the entire world—not part of it, but all of it. He is anxious to demonstrate his invention before someone else beats him to it and secures all the credit. At the end of the play, he and his wife stand lovingly together, their fingers in their ears; as she sweetly coos, "Goodbye, love. And congratulations," he blows up the world. The absurdly elephantine title *Oh Dad, Poor Dad, Mamma's Hung You in the Closet and I'm Feelin' So Sad* is appropriate for a grotesque satire on American Moms, featuring a Philip Wylie monster mother, a frightened son who has been prevented from maturing, a pretty girl who unsuccessfully tries to remedy this lack, and a stuffed corpse (the "Poor Dad" of the title) who falls out of the bedroom closet onto the bodies of the boy

and girl at an extremely inconvenient moment. However, *Oh Dad,
etc.* is at the same time a parody on French *avant-garde* drama.
One of the difficulties with the play, I think, is that Kopit has not
adequately connected the serious satire on Momism and the play-
ful spoof on the *avant-garde.*

So far, the new American playwrights of the off-Broadway
scene appear to be either Minor League players trying to crack the
Majors uptown (and sometimes succeeding) or bedfellows of the
School of Paris. But there is another group of playwrights whose
work fits into neither of these categories and who seem to have
achieved a uniquely American identity together with a loose unity
with each other in terms of a common desire to portray realistically the reality they see around them, a common dissatisfaction
with the techniques of the commercial play, and similar experimentation with new techniques. I would like to concentrate on what
appears to be the significant works of these playwrights: Jack Gelber's *The Connection,* Kenneth Brown's *The Brig,* and LeRoi Jones'
Dutchman. But first it would be useful to examine the milieu in
which these plays were presented and for which they were written.

When one visits an off-Broadway theatre one is aware of several differences from a Broadway house. For one thing, the tickets
are cheaper. For another, the usherettes are usually younger and
prettier. The candy vendors have less polish. (I remember one such
vendor, hawking assorted chocolates during an intermission, calling
out, "Sordid chocolates.") The theatres are smaller. The facilities—
stage, backstage, auditorium, and restrooms—are more primitive.
Off-Broadway houses present a less austere, a less forbidding atmosphere than Broadway houses, and a closer relationship between the
audience and the actors. Part of this stems from the smallness
of the theatres and the greater physical proximity between stage and
auditorium. The audience is *literally* closer to the events on stage.
But at the same time the audience is aware that it is a *stage*
which it is closer to. We have, then, the potential for greater
realism and, simultaneously, a potential trouble spot, for one of the
biggest problems of stage realism, as Arthur Hopkins pointed out
almost half a century ago in a discussion of stage scenery, is that
an accurate stage reproduction of reality is self-defeating since it is
remarkable only because it is not real, and that it therefore calls
attention to the unreality of the whole enterprise. With this in mind,
let us analyze the plays I have mentioned. These plays comprise
what might be called The New Realism, for although they are

realistic plays, they are different from the realism of Ibsen, Hauptmann, Chayefsky, and Wesker.

The Connection is a play about dope addicts. Usually, this sort
of drama is either a tale of a courageous junkie who kicks the
habit (substitute the word "booze" for the word "pot" and you
can easily see the kinship with the melodramas of yester-year) or
else a psychological study of human frailty which pleads for compassionate understanding. For Gelber, both of these approaches are
"square," and he satirizes the old-fashioned drama when one of his
characters assures the audience that The Connection does not conclude—as, by the way, A Hatful of Rain does conclude—with a
housewife calling the police and asking them to come immediately
to the theatre because her husband is a junkie. Gelber uses narcotics addiction as a metaphor for that connection which we all
need to enable us to go on living. There are no basic differences
between the junkies we see on stage waiting for their connection to
arrive and give them a fix, and the respectable people in the audience who (probably) have a legal and more socially acceptable
connection. The man who arrives with the narcotics, Cowboy (so
named, I suppose, because he comes with "horse"), reminds one
of the addict who has condemned the "daytime" people for being
"square" and not "hip," that there is nothing wrong with having a
day job, that there are good and bad hipsters as well as good and
bad squares, and that although he could not tolerate a daily work job
since he prefers his hours as they are, this does not make him
better than the daytime people. Neither, it is implied, does it make
him essentially different from the daytime people. Some people need
a vitamin pill, others a new coat, a new car, reassurance from an
analyst, or reassurance from a minister—there are numerous socially
approved connections. As Solly, the wise (Solomon-like) junkie, puts
it, each fix that we wait for, that we desperately need, whatever that fix may be, is "a fix of hope. A fix to forget. A fix to
remember, to be sad, to be happy, to be, to be." We all, Gelber
is saying, take some form of dope.

It is society's unwillingness to acknowledge this, and to con-
demn or (what is in some respects worse) to condescendingly pity
the narcotics addicts, that constitutes one of Gelber's major themes
and certainly his major accusation. In addition to Cowboy's ironic
condescension to us in the passage I have paraphrased, there are
characters in the play who represent the respectable world; moreover, that world is actually present in the auditorium. During the

course of the play, two of the representatives of the world of respectability are drawn into the world of the drug addicts. By having them take dope, Gelber dramatizes the bond between both worlds. But Gelber is also concerned with the actual members of the respectable world, the audience.

As we enter the auditorium we see that the curtain is already up. The realistic stage setting looks as though it needs to be disinfected. There are people in that setting, we notice. Actors? Or are they bums who have wandered in out of the street? Of course they must be actors. But they too appear to be in need of fumigation. They recline on a bed or are slumped over a table or wander about aimlessly. One of them plays a few bars on a piano or beats a snare drum a few times, then gives it up as a worthless activity. One of them occasionally glances at us as if we were a necessary evil to be tolerated. Another furtively peeks at us, then looks away with loathing. We begin to feel uncomfortable. The performance, we realize later (some of us realize now), has already begun; and we are in it. A "producer" appears, welcomes us to the theatre, and introduces the "author" of the evening's entertainment. He speaks to us in language that reveals him as the square trying to be hip, and some of us feel still more uncomfortable, for this is our language. He tells us that the author (named Jaybird, an appropriate tag for this foolish, gullible young man) has lived among dope addicts for a few months in order to understand them. We learn, too, that Jaybird has written character biographies and some form of scenario for what will be an improvised performance. We are told smilingly that this improvisation will be performed by real dope addicts, whose payment for the evening's enterainment will be, we are also told smilingly, a fix. In order to calm the more apprehensive members of the audience before we enter the lobby during the interval, the producer assures us that this fix—to be given during the second act—will be a "scientifically accurate amount of heroin." The discomfort we felt at the beginning of the performance is intensified. If these are real addicts assembled for our amusement, what does that make us, who pay for the dose? We are not allowed to forget this. On a few occasions (just enough to make us remember), we are reminded of this explicitly. In the first act one of the junkies, waiting for Cowboy to arrive with the heroin, savagely indicts the audience, "I really don't believe any of you understand what this is about. You're stupid. Why are you here? Because you want to see someone suffer. You want to laugh at me? You don't want to know me." And in the second act, after Cowboy has arrived, another junkie, who has just been turned on, tells us in a more jovial manner, "I want to take the opportunity to thank each and every kind, gentle, and good contributor in the audience. You have helped a most noble cause that is dear to our hearts. That goodness, that goodness that flows in our veins is the evidence—is the evidence of our gratitude toward you and every one of our fellow men."

The pattern of the play is straightforward: in the first act, the addicts wait for Cowboy to bring the dope. Just before the act ends he is seen through the window. During the second act the junkies are turned on. One of them, who has not received his "kick" from the drug, gives himself a second fix (on stage!) that proves to be an overdose and that almost kills him. Also during the second act, the playwright and one of two cameramen who have arrived to film the events are persuaded to get a fix. These two—who have been sitting in our midst in the auditorium during most of the action—establish the physical link between our world and the world of the junkies. As Jaybird himself puts it at the end of the play, "Well, if it wasn't junk, I would have been involved with something else."

I call Gelber's play an example of The New Realism. I do not do so because he uses a group of social outcasts to symbolize social incasts; after all, Gorky did this in *The Lower Depths*. Nor do I use the term because he is leveling an attack upon his audience; Shaw did this in *Mrs. Warren's Profession*. One of the things which makes Gelber's play so unique as realism is that he uses so many devices of the non-realistic theatre. Consider: the "author" is introduced to the audience; the "producer" tells us that what we will see has no naturalistic basis; a character enters and asks whether the play has begun; actors go into the auditorium and later return to the stage; the "producer" stops the action of the play to introduce the cast to the audience; the "author" complains that the actors are not following his story and has an argument with them; several characters address us directly; one character announces that he will panhandle from us during the interval, and he does; etc. If these devices remind us of anyone, they remind us not of any of the naturalistic playwrights but of Pirandello! And Gelber's practice is indeed Pirandellian. He audaciously—and successfully, I think—uses theatricality to make us believe that we are watching reality. In *The Connection*, the basic

set-up is not actors who are going to play junkies, but junkies
who are going to try to be actors. Therefore, whenever we are reminded that we are in a theatre looking at a stage, we are at
the same time reminded that we are looking at non-actors. The
theatricalism enforces the realism to create a slice of life that is
much more successful than might have been achieved if Gelber had
tried "straight" realism. Hopkins' objection to realism is circum-
vented for Gelber directs his audience's attention to the unreality
he wants them to focus on in order to divert their attention from
the unreality he wants to hide: namely, that actors are playing
junkies playing actors.

Kenneth Tynan called *The Connection* the most exciting new
American play produced off-Broadway since World War II. I agree,
and it is mainly because of Gelber's remarkable accomplishment that
I have spent so much time on this play. The other major plays
of The New Realism that I am going to discuss—*The Brig* and
Dutchman—are, I think, important but less successful.

The Brig, a grim enactment of life in a Marine Corps prison
written by an ex-marine, Kenneth Brown, uses none of the theat-
ricalist devices of *The Connection*. Heavy chicken-wire separates
the stage from the audience. The audience stays on its side of
the chicken-wire, the actors on theirs. The play has no plot. It is
a series of six scenes comprising a typical day in a Marine Corps
prison, beginning at 4:00 A.M., shortly before the prisoners are
officially awakened, and ending with "Lights Out." During this typical day, we are exposed to the brutality and bestiality of life in
the brig. Prisoners are designated not by name but by a number,
or else they are called "maggots" and "worms." Prisoners are not
allowed to walk but must run or trot. Before doing anything or
saying anything, they must loudly request permission to do it or
say it: "sir, prisoner number Ten"—or whatever his number is—
"requests permission to speak, sir." If the prisoner adds "please,"
he is reprimanded and made to repeat his request. If the guard
does not think the request was made in a sufficiently loud voice,
he demands that it be repeated until the decibels satisfy him. A
white line marks every entrance and exit—between the cells and
the corridor, between one corridor and another, between the Turn-
key's area and the compound, etc. Whenever a prisoner wishes
to cross a white line he must request permission to do so. If he
crosses without permission he is beaten. In fact, he may be beaten
at any time and for any reason at all.

These beatings are a constantly recurring feature of life in the brig. Here is a typical example. Sease, one of the guards, calls to a prisoner who is about to distribute shovels to four other prisoners.

> Nineteen, you crossed my white line without asking me first.
> Tonight is your night, nineteen.
> *SEASE gets up and walks to NINETEEN.*
> Now give each worm his shovel.
> *NINETEEN hands a shovel to each prisoner.*
> *SEASE punches NINETEEN in the stomach.*
> Tonight is your night, nineteen.
> *Pause.*
> Get out, maggots.
> *The four PRISONERS disappear . . . .*

The repeated beatings, the references to human beings as numbers or as maggots, the incessant requests for permission to cross white lines—these accumulate into steadily mounting images of humanity dehumanized and subhumanized. They reach a terrifying emotional climax when one of the prisoners cracks up, shouts that his name is not Twenty-six but James Turner, and is put into a strait jacket and removed. Following this scene, however, is the quieter but more frightening final episode: a new prisoner is brought in and is shown the ropes. The pattern repeats itself.

More is involved than a cumulative series of scenes in a torture factory. First, the picture is an accurate one. Second, as with *The Connection*, we are indicted and are made acutely uncomfortable by the spectacle. If this is dehumanized life, then we, who tolerate or are silent in the face of such barbarism, are even more inhuman than the guards in the play. In addition, against as with *The Connection*, the events on stage serve as metaphor for a larger issue. We, too, Brown seems to imply, exist in an insecure and often totalitarian world in which the sky can come crashing down on us and we can be destroyed by the most minor infraction of totally arbitrary rules. Finally, the play achieves a direct, non-literary, kinesthetic communication with us. Not only does the violence affect our very muscles, but the repetition of phrases, of sentences, of movements, and of the violence itself creates an insinuating rhythm that provokes a direct experience of the cruelty that occurs on stage.

This is more than documentary realism, though it is also that. The very pulse of the plan is transmitted to the audience. Another aspect of this New Realism that distinguishes it from the older type is the abandonment of traditional features of play construction. Indeed, some have called *The Brig* not a play at all but a literal reenactment of military prison life. Although it is true that *The Brig* does not have a plot but instead has a group of incidents related by a common theme, locale, and characters, it is not a literal reenactment; instead it is a series of scenes whose basic rhythms are repeated and built in such a way as to force a direct, kinesthetic response from the audience.

In terms of the rejection of conventional dramaturgy—the use of a cycle to suggest recurrence and deadly inevitability, the attack upon the audience linked with a direct assault upon its senses and emotions, the presentation of an unsavory segment of American life, and the use of this segment to serve as metaphor for a larger area not only of American life but of Western life—*The Brig* appears to be following the general lines of *The Connection. Dutchman,* by the Negro poet, LeRoi Jones, also appears to be following these general lines.

Dutchman, whose title may be an ironic reference to the Wagnerian opera, is a one-act paean of hate. A thirty-year-old, sexy, neurotic White woman gets on a subway train, sits next to a twenty-year-old Negro, and gives him what looks like a come-on. She alternately speaks seductively to him, ignores him, grabs his thigh, and insults him. One begins to wonder—along with the Negro boy—whether she is quite sane. At one moment she looks him in the eye and talks of unbuttoning her dress and letting her skirt fall; the next moment she calls him "black nigger." The boy is embarrassed and does not know what to make of her strange behavior, but at the same time he is reluctant to pass up what looks like a wild evening. Her overtures become more obviously erotic: she sings, dances, tries to persuade him to dance with her, and finally calls on him to make love to her right then and there. His refusal prompts a violent reaction. She mocks him, curses him, and tries to humiliate him. As she taunts him, the other subway riders laugh. The Negro, provoked at last, thrusts her into her seat and slaps her to shut her up. Then, in a flood of rhetorical venom, he pours out the hatred he has for her and every White. His White Man's three-button suit, he says, is a disguise to keep him from cutting the White Man's throat; the White Man does not know that Bessie Smith and Charlie Parker—whom he idolizes —hated him, that Bessie sang and Bird played in order to hide their hate, and that these very performances became acts of hate. In the heart of every Negro, he tells her, is hatred for every White, and this hatred will one day become murder. She then takes out a knife and stabs him. She orders the other riders to throw his body out of the train and to get off at the next stop. They obey. She scribbles a note in a notebook. Another twenty-year-old Negro enters. She looks at him provocatively.

Dutchman might be described as a realistic play with the motivation left out. This is one element which distinguishes it from traditionally realistic plays. For Jones, what the White woman does is more important than why she does it. Although her actions are believable, her motivation is not spelled out. Antonin Artaud, spokesman for a theatre that would create subliminal shocks and that would forcefully convey to the spectators a sense of the cruelty of existence, wanted the theatrical experience to leave an ineffaceable scar. LeRoi Jones, by concentrating on the social attitudes and actions created by unstated motivations, and at the same time making the sensuality and violence a direct sensory and emotional experience, goes at least some distance toward realizing that aim. *Dutchman* may not leave an ineffacable scare—far from it—but it does create a considerable shock. This may be said not only of Dutchman but also of *The Brig* and *The Connection.* All three plays blend an attack on the values of the audience with an attack on its senses and emotions in order to create a direct theatrical experience.

From the unadorned dialogue of Samuel Beckett to the almost baroque splendor of Jean Genet's language, European playwrights are creating various dramatic visions which constitute what Martin Eselin has called The Theatre of the Absurd. The major experimental playwrights of the United States are pursuing their own visions and do not, in the main, appear to be tormented by The Absurdity of the Human Condition. This may be a blessing, for the concept has become a cliché. Nevertheless, they are responding to the cruelty of existence as they see it inside themselves and as they find it reflected in the world around them at a particular moment of history—Jones, showing the tensions of the Negro in the White Man's world; Brown, portraying the inhumanity of a totalitarian system; Gelber, presenting man lost and alone, trying to make a connection with something which, if it will not give his life meaning, will at least enable him to go on living. John Osborne's febrile protagonist of *Look Back in Anger*, Jimmy Porter, complains at one point that he is living in the American Age. Whether or not this is cause for complaint depends upon one's point of view. But in many respects Jimmy Porter is right, and whatever one's point of view may be, our major experimental playwrights, in presenting dramatic images of fears and tensions of their world, are speaking out not only for a vital segment of the United States but for a vital segment of the rest of the Western world as well.

Bibliographical Notes

With the exception of the essays on Tennessee Williams and Edward Albee, the bibliographical notes were prepared by the authors of the essays. Reviews of *Blues for Mr. Charlie* will be found in the popular magazines such as *Commonweal, The New Republic, Nation, The New Yorker, The Saturday Review,* etc., for the years 1964 and 1965; of *The Member of the Wedding* for the year 1950; of *The Square Root of Wonderful* for the years 1957 and 1958; and of *The Last Analysis* for the year 1964. The essay on the Off-Broadway Theater is reprinted from a talk given by Professor Dukore over the Voice of America.

WET

EUGENE O'NEILL

The most complete collection of O'Neill's plays is the three-volume edition published by Random House in 1941 under the title, *The Plays of Eugene O'Neill* (New York; reissued 1951 with *The Iceman Cometh* added in volume 3). *A Moon for the Misbegotten* was published separately in 1952 by Random House, which also publishes cheaper reprints of many of the plays in its Modern Library series. After an altercation concerning the publication of *Long Day's Journey into Night,* O'Neill's widow and literary executrix, Carlotta Monterey O'Neill, transferred rights to the disputed play and all subsequently published plays to the Yale University Press, which has since issued *Long Day's Journey* (1956), *A Touch of the Poet* (1957), *More Stately Mansions* (1964; shortened from the author's partly revised script by Karl Ragnar Gierow and edited by Donald Gallup), and the one-act play *Hughie* (1959). Most of the Yale editions are available in paperback.

The now standard biography is *O'Neill* by Arthur and Barbara Gelb (New York: Harper and Row, 1962), a massive work containing much detailed information and some literary criticism. Croswell Bowen's *The Curse of the Misbegotten* is much shorter and more sensationalistic and is largely superseded by the Gelbs' biography except for such light as it sheds upon O'Neill's younger son, Shane, who the author says assisted in the writing. Barrett H. Clark was the first to offer a critical biography of O'Neill, and since its original publication in 1926 the book has been several times revised as *Eugene O'Neill: The Man and His Plays* (New York: McBride, 1929, 1933, 1936; New York, Dover, 1947). Clark enjoyed O'Neill's interest and cooperation but apparently had to submit to his editing of the work as well. O'Neill's second wife, Agnes Boulton, has written about some of her life with the playwright in *Part of a Long Story* (New York: Doubleday, 1958).

There is no dearth of criticism on O'Neill's plays, ranging from opening night reviews to full-length books. Many reviews, articles, biographical notes, and reprints of O'Neill's own non-dramatic writings have been collected in *O'Neill and His Plays: Four Decades of Criticism,* edited by Oscar Cargill, N. Bryllion Fagin, and William J. Fisher (New York: New York University Press, 1961). This volume also contains several appendices on the first performances and publications of O'Neill's plays in addition to an extensive bibliography, all of which I have found extremely useful. The editors cite Doris Falk's *Eugene O'Neill and the Tragic Vision: An Interpretive Study of the Plays* (New Brunswick: Rutgers, 1958) as "the best critical volume in English to date," but unfortunately I have been unable to consult it during the time of composing my own essay. F. I. Carpenter has contributed a critical study in Twayne's United States Authors Series, *Eugene O'Neill* (New York, 1964), and the English critic and scholar, Clifford Leech, has written illuminatingly on *The Iceman Cometh* in a handy little book, *Eugene O'Neill* (Edinburgh: Oliver and Boyd, 1963; New York: Grove Press). Another recent full length study of the man and his work is John Henry Raleigh's *Eugene O'Neill* (Carbondale:

Southern Illinois Press, 1965). The best single article on the late plays that I have consulted is Tom F. Driver's "On the Late Plays of Eugene O'Neill," *Tulane Drama Review*, III (December 1958), 8-20. This essay is reprinted along with a number of other excellent pieces in *O'Neill: A Collection of Critical Essays*, edited by John Gassner for Twentieth Century Views (Englewood Cliffs, N. J.: Prentice Hall, 1964).

CLIFFORD ODETS

Full Length Studies.

The only full length study that has been published on Clifford Odets is R. Baird Shuman's *Clifford Odets,* volume 30 of Twayne's United States Authors Series (New York: 1962). This book limits itself to a consideration of Odets' published plays and is based on Mr. Shuman's doctoral dissertation, *Social Concepts in the Stage Plays of Clifford Odets* (University of Pennsylvania: 1961). Other valuable full length studies which have not been published are Arthur Wagner's *Technique in the Revolutionary Plays of Clifford Odets* (Stanford University: 1962) which offers penetrating insights into the structure of the early plays; Michael Mendelsohn's *Clifford Odets: A Critical Study* (University of Colorado: 1963) which is the most comprehensive study extant of Odets' work, considering not only the published plays, but the movies, radio scripts, and unpublished plays as well; and David Kuryk's *Love's Thin Awkward Plant: A Study of the Work of Clifford Odets in Regard to the Individual and His Relationship to Society* (University of Wisconsin: 1965) which is a sensitively written consideration of Odets' work viewed largely from a sociological viewpoint. Richard E. Wilson's unpublished master's thesis, *A Director's Production Book for Clifford Odets' The Flowering Peach* (Stanford University: 1959), while limited in scope, presents valuable biographical information in the first chapter and gives penetrating commentary on Odets' last play to be produced.

Books.

Block, Anita. *The Changing World in Plays and Theatre.* Boston: Little, Brown and Company, 1939. Miss Block presents a realistic view of Odets' relationship to the social forces which motivated his writing.

Clurman, Harold. *The Fervent Years: The Story of the Group Theatre and the Thirties.* New York: Alfred A. Knopf, 1945. Much of Odets' growth as a playwright is chronicled in this book by his close friend and associate.

Dusenbury, Winifred L. *The Theme of Loneliness in Modern American Drama.* Gainesville: University of Florida Press, 1960. Dusenbury relates Odets' early plays, through *Night Music,* to the theme of loneliness. Good commentary on the personal isolation theme in the plays.

Krutch, Joseph Wood. *American Drama Since 1918: An Informal History.* New York: George Braziller, Inc., 1957. Krutch thoughtfully relates Odets to the rise of realism in American writing during the '30s.

Lawson, John Howard. *Theory and Technique of Playwriting.* New York: Hill and Wang, 1960. Lawson concerns himself with the structural elements in Odets' early plays. His observations are cogent.

Nannes, Casper. *Politics in the American Drama as Revealed by Plays Produced on the New York Stage, 1890-1945.* Philadelphia: University of Pennsylvania Press, 1950. Republished and expanded in 1960 as *Politics in the American Drama* (Washington: The Catholic University of America Press). The best evaluation in print of Odets' *Till the Day I Die.*

O'Hara, Frank. *Today in American Drama.* Chicago: University of Chicago Press, 1939. Chapter V gives good insights on social drama and Odets' relationship to it.

Articles.

Brustein, Robert. "America's New Culture-Hero: Feeling without Words." *Commentary,* XXV (February, 1958), 123-129. Comments on the verbal coherence of the proletarian heroes in the plays of authors like Odets.

Fagin, N. B. "In Search of an American *Cherry Orchard.*" *Texas Quarterly,* I (Summer-Aumumn, 1958), 132. Comments on the theory, discounted by Odets, that he was strongly influenced by Chekhov. Concludes that the influence was only of the most general and universal nature.

Gassner, John. "The Long Journey of Talent." *Theatre Arts Monhtly,* XXXIII (July, 1949), 26-131. Comments on the fact that Odets' time in Hollywood did not eviscerate him as an author.

Hughes, Catharine. "Odets: The Price of Success." *Commonweal,* LXXVIII (1963), 558-560. Laments the waning of Odets' literary activity as his plays won him recognition.

McCarten, John. "Revolution's Number One Boy." *The New Yorker,* XIV (January 22, 1938), 21-27. This is the standard early biographical article on Odets.

Mendelsohn, Michael. "Clifford Odets and the American Family." *Drama Survey,* III (1963), 238-243. Especially valuable for it comments on *Awake and Sing!* and *Paradise Lost.*

—. "Clifford Odets: the Artist's Commitment." *Literature and Society* [12], 142-152. Very revealing in terms of Odets' personal struggle to maintain his artistic integrity and ideals in the years after he left Broadway.

Shuman, R. Baird. "*Waiting for Lefty*: A Problem in Structure." *Revue des Langues Vivantes,* XXVIII (1962), 521-526. While limited to a single play, this article views the conscious artistry of Odets.

[Wagner, Arthur.] "How a Playwright Triumphs." *Harper's,* CCXXXIII (September, 1966), 64-74. This article, based on interviews with Odets shortly before his death, is one of the most valuable pieces of writing on the author. An exceptionally objective approach on Mr. Wagner's part.

A full length study of Odets is to be published soon by Mrs. William Gibson. Of interest also is William Gibson's preface to *Golden Boy* (New York: Bantam Books, 1966) entitled "A Memento." This brief essay tells of Odets' final days.

MAXWELL ANDERSON

Maxwell Anderson was not an innovator in dramatic technique, but he felt the need to explain, if not to defend, his practice, so he wrote and published a small book of essays called *Off-Broadway* (New York: W. Sloane Associates, 1947). Three chapters of the book that are especially interesting are "Poetry in the Theater," "The Essence of Tragedy," and "The Uses of Poetry." On the basis of this book, which she felt had been too long neglected, Mabel Driscoll Bailey wrote an analysis of Anderson's plays, *The Playwright as Prophet* (New York: Abelard-Schuman, 1957), which is a sympathetic and sometimes enthusiastic analysis of how Maxwell Anderson's aesthetic is expressed in the plays. Especially interesting is her defense of Anderson's dramatic poetry in the title chapter of the book.

Joseph Wood Krutch has dealt with Anderson in two of his books about the theater. In *The American Drama Since 1918* (New York: George Braziller, Inc., 1957) he suggests that Anderson's stature in American drama approaches that of O'Neill. Krutch defends the poetry, especially in *Winterset* and *High Tor*, saying it "limbers up the imagination." He further points out that Anderson's traditionalism is a healthy counter to Marxian tendencies in the theater of the 30's.

Perhaps John Mason Brown states best the ambivalent way critics generally react to Anderson. Negatively, Brown, in *Dramatis Personae* (New York: The Viking Press, 1963), feels rather strongly that Anderson was unable to create a verse that suited his characters and action. He speaks of purple patches. On the other hand, Brown is strongly drawn to Anderson's nobility and his insistence that the theater can still provide an elevating and tragic experience.

Edmund M. Gagey, in *Revolution in American Drama* (New York: Columbia University Press, 1947) has a chapter on poetry and imagination, in which he points out Anderson's traditionalism, his drawing upon Elizabethan subjects for his tragedies and on *Hamlet, Lear,* and *Romeo and Juliet* for the plot of *Winterset*. He further discusses the social protest and satire in both *Valley Forge* and *Winterset*.

John Gassner, *The Theatre in Our Times* (New York: Crown Publishers, Inc., 1954), sees Anderson as one of the "rebuilders" of the drama, after the destructive influences of such dramatists as Strindberg and Pirandello. He makes an interesting case for Anderson's integrity as a "poet in show business" and suggests that even so Anderson "has employed every avant-garde device at some time or other."

Finally, Stark Young, in *Immortal Shadows* (New York: Hill & Wang, 1948), makes a perceptive analysis of the complex characterization of George Washington in Anderson's *Valley Forge*.

COMEDY OF MANNERS

A perceptive and reliable study of modern comedy in the American theatre occurs in *The American Drama Since 1918* by Joseph Wood Krutch, New York, 1939. *American Playwrights: 1918-1938* by Eleanor Flexner, New York, 1938, is also a valuable work, partly because it is a penetrating analysis of playwriting from the point of view of the sociological criticism of the 1930s. *The Theatre in Our Times* by John Gassner has chapters on Barry, Sherwood, and Behrman. Written by an author who has vast knowledge of the modern theatre, they are readable and revealing. *The American Theatre 1752-1934,* edited by Montrose J. Moses and John Mason Brown, New York, 1934, is an admirable collection of theatre criticism by critics ranging from Washington Irving to Brooks Atkinson. Useful for the student of the theatre are the reviews or collections of reviews by such distinguished critics as George Jean Nathan (see his *Theatre of the Moment,* New York, 1936); John Mason Brown (see his *Upstage: The American Theatre in Performance,* New York, 1930); and Brooks Atkinson (see his *Broadway Scrapbook,* New York, 1947). Useful as a reference work about plays produced in New York is the series entitled *The Best Plays and the Year Book of the Drama in America* formerly edited by Burns Mantle, now edited by Henry Hewes, New York. For the complete texts of selected plays from 1916 to 1965 see the excellent series of volumes entitled *Best American Plays* edited by John Gassner, New York. There have been several notable periodicals devoted to the drama. One of the most valuable for reference and criticism of the period discussed in this chapter is *Theatre Arts Monthly* in publication from January, 1924, to October, 1939. So also is the magazine *Vanity Fair* which ran from 1914 to 1936. It is a rich compendium of artistic and literary materials for the cultural historian. (See the single volume of selections from *Vanity Fair* edited by Cleveland Amory and Frederic Bradlee, New York, 1960.) Of continuing interest to the student of comedy are two classic works, *Laughter* by Henri Bergson and *Essay on Comedy* by George Meredith. These are available in a single paperback volume containing a supplementary essay and Introduction by Wylie Sypher and published by Doubleday & Company, Garden City, New York.

TENNESSEE WILLIAMS

An impressive bibliography of Tennessee Williams studies has been accumulating since Williams' success in the 1940's. He has himself written an essay about almost all his plays, and of course, the New York drama critics have reviewed his plays, commenting either favorably or unfavorably. Brooks Atkinson has probably been one of Williams' staunchest defenders, though Harold Clurman, George Jean Nathan, John Mason Brown, and others have had some favorable things to say.

Eric Bentley, always a perceptive critic, has raised some interesting questions about Williams' work in "Camino Unreal," in *The Dramatic Event* (Boston: Beacon Press, 1954), such as the "hash Williams has made out of D. H. Lawrence," and the relationship between Williams and Elia Kazan. He has pursued this latter matter in *What is Theatre* (Boston: Beacon Press, 1956). Stark Young, in *Immortal Shadows* (N. Y.: Hill and Wang, 1948), was an early critic to recognize Williams' mastery of a poetic language and a poetic theater. John Gassner, in "Tennessee Williams: Dramatist of Frustration" (*College English,* October, 1948); Joseph Wood Krutch in *Modernism in Modern Drama* (N. Y.: Cornell University Press, 1953); and Henry Popkin, in "The Plays of Tennessee Williams" (*Tulane Drama Review,* March, 1960) have all made contributions to our understanding of the dramatist.

Several book-length studies of Williams have been made. Some of them are:

Donahue, Francis. *The Dramatic World of Tennessee Williams.* N. Y.: Frederick Ungar Publishing Co., 1964.

Falk, Signi. *Tennessee Williams.* New Haven, Conn.: College and University Press (Twayne's United States Authors Series), 1961.

Jackson, Esther Merle. *The Broken World of Tennessee Williams.* Madison, Wisconsin: The University of Wisconsin Press, 1966.
Nelson, Benjamin. *Tennessee Williams: The Man and His Work,* New York: Ivan Obolensky, Inc., 1961.

Tischler, Nancy M. *Tennessee Williams: Rebelious Puritan*. New York: The Citadel Press, 1961.

ARTHUR MILLER

For an excellent comprehensive listing of Miller's works, including unpublished plays, and of the major Miller criticism in periodical articles and reviews up to 1961, see: Martha Turnquist Eissenstat, "Arthur Miller: A Bibliography," *Modern Drama*, vol. 5, no. 1 (May, 1962), pp. 93-106; also, Robert G. Shedd, "Modern Drama: A Selective Bibliography of Works Published in English in 1963-64," *MD*, vol. 18, no. 2 (September, 1965), pp. 224-225; Shedd, "Modern Drama: A Selective Bibliography of Works Published in English in 1965," *MD*, vol. 9, no. 2 (September, 1966), p. 225. And these individual works: Arthur Ganz, "The Silence of Arthur Miller," *Drama Survey*, vol. 3, no. 2 (October, 1963), pp. 224-237; Ganz, "Arthur Miller: After the Silence," *DS*, vol. 3, no. 4 (Spring-Fall, 1964), pp. 520-530; John V. Hagopian, "Arthur Miller: *The Salesman's Two Cases*," *MD*, vol. 6, no. 2 (September, 1963), pp. 117-125; Emile G. McAnany, S. J., "The Tragic Commitment: Some Notes on Arthur Miller," *MD*, vol. 5, no. 1 (May, 1962), pp. 11-20; Leonard Moss, "Arthur Miller and the Common Man's Language," *MD*, vol. 7, no. 1 (May, 1964), pp. 52-59.

THREE VERSE PLAYWRIGHTS AND THE AMERICAN FIFTIES

As might be expected, given the situation in American verse drama, the body of criticism dealing with the subject is equally limited. Many of the available comments on the verse plays are buried in books about the authors of the verse plays, books which consider the author primarily as a poet, though, and correspondingly treat his dramatic material as if it were poetry. The following bibliography is highly selective in that it attempts to note only those studies which are willing to treat the dramatic work of the three verse playwrights under consideration as separate entities.

(For a general study of the situation in the American verse theater before the 50's, see my article "Verse Drama in America: 1916-1939," *Modern Drama* VI (December, 1963), 309-322.)

DJUNA BARNES

Barnes, Djuna. *The Antiphon.* New York: Farrar, Straus & Cudahy, 1958.

Abel, Lionel. *Metatheatre: A New View of Dramatic Form.* New York: Hill and Wang, 1963. In an essay "Bad by North and South" cast in the form of a dramatic dialogue, Abel records his unfavorable reaction to *The Antiphon* and to *J. B.*

London Times Literary Supplement, April 1958, p. 182. "A Daughter for Inquisitor" is a highly complimentary review of Barnes' play within the limits of the assumption that it is really a poem.

Ponsot, Marie. *Careful Sorrow and Observed Compline,"* Poetry, XCV: (October, 1959), 47-50.

RICHARD EBERHART

Eberhart, Richard. *The Visionary Farms* in *New World Writing* 3. New York: New American Library, 1953, pp. 63-97.

——————————, "Tragedy as Limitation: Comedy as Control and Resolution," *Tulane Drama Review* VI (June, 1962), 3-14. Eberhart talks about his intentions and conceptions in *The Visionary Farms*. This issue also prints the texts of "Devils and "Angels" and "The Mad Musicians" as part of a section devoted to The Theatre of Richard Eberhart.

ARCHIBALD MACLEISH

MacLeish, Archibald. *J. B.* Boston: Houghton Mifflin, 1958.
—————————. *This Music Crept by Me Upon the Waters.* Cambridge, Mass.: Harvard University Press, 1953.
—————. *The Trojan Horse.* Boston: Houghton Mifflin, 1952.

Abel, Lionel. *Metatheatre.* See under BARNES.

Casper, Leonard. "The God Mask of MacLeish," *Drama Critique I* (November, 1958), 11-12. Casper finds the play shallow, a cliche.

Christensen, Parley A. *"J. B.,* the Critics and Me," *Western Humanities Review* XV (Spring, 1961), 111-126. A reading of the play within its own context, despite the theological confusions that critics have found.

Falk, Signi Lenea. *Archibald MacLeish*. New York: Twayne Publishers, 1965. In a general study of MacLeish's achievement, his verse drama receives a relatively small amount of attention.

Grebstein, Sheldon. "*J. B.* and the Problems of Evil," *University of Kansas City Review* XXIX (June, 1963), 253-261.

Kazan, Elia, and Archibald MacLeish, "The Staging of a Play," *Esquire*, LI (May, 1959), 144-146; 148-158. Notes and letters which indicate the transformation which took place during production of *J. B.*

MacLeish, Andrew. "*J. B.* and the Critics," *Modern Drama* II (December, 1959), 224-230.

MacLeish, Archibald. "The Men Behind J. B., *Theatre Arts* XLI (April, 1959), 60-63. MacLeish testifies to the humanistic basis of his play.

Sickels, Eleanor M. "MacLeish and the Fortunate Fall," *American Literature* XXXV (May, 1963), 205-217.

Stock, Ely. "*A Masque of Reason* and *J. B.*: Two Treatments of the *Book of Job*," *Modern Drama* III (February, 1961), 378-386. An examination and comparison of Robert Frost's *Masque of Reason* with *J. B.*, which concludes that Frost's masque is closer to the original.

EDWARD ALBEE

Edward Albee has defended his plays, particularly *Who's Afraid of Virginia Woolf?*, in an essay that originally appeared in the *New York Times Magazine* for February 25, 1962. It was called "Which Theater is the Absurd One?" and it concludes that the theater which produces Ionesco, Brecht, Genet, and Beckett is the real theater, and the commercial theater, pandering to popular taste, is the truly absurd one. Martin Esslin, author of *The Theatre of the Absurd* (Anchor, 1961), includes Albee in his discussion of these existentialist playwrights, and he has generally been considered one of them since. Certainly, Albee's defense of his plays was called for. The reviewers have for the most part received his plays with either complete disbelief, anger, or disgust, though his reputation among some critics has become more than respectable. For example, Ray Irwin, in "Who's Afraid of Virginia Woolf, Hunh?" (*Atlantic Monthly*, Vol. 213, April 1964, p. 122; 124) made a frontal and not very subtle attack on the language in Albee's play. Resenting Albee's making the characters in *Who's Afraid* . . . college professors and their wives, Irwin says: "I feel no obligation to marshal evidence that Mr. Albee doesn't know what the hell he's talking about." On the other hand, Alfred Chester, in "Edward Albee: Red Herring & White Whales" in *Commentary*, Vol. 35 (April, 1863), pp. 296-301, attacks the play from the standpoint of structure, accusing Albee of playwrighting trickery by pulling the "son" out of the hat at the end of the play, thereby "lifting" the action and the characters into total negation.

Diana Trilling, in "Who's Afraid of The Culturally Elite?," in *Esquire*, Vol. XL, No. 6 (December, 1963), pp. 69-88, takes a somewhat less critical attitude toward the play and approaches it from the viewpoint of the audience's reactions to it. She wonders why the audiences fill the theater every night and go away raving about the play, while the reviewers generally have panned it. Her conclusion is startling. *Who's Afraid* . . . is popular because it takes an intellectually uninitiated audience into the groves of academe and grants them intellectual "status." Marya Mannes, "The Half-world of American Drama," *The Republic*, Vol. 28 (April 25, 1963) rounds out this bibliographical note by placing Albee's play in perspective by relating it to the Off-Broadway Theater and its playwrights and by suggesting that Albee's great talent needs to grow until he can paint larger canvasses and deal with themes of greater depth than he has yet been able to manage.

About the Contributors

Benard F. Dukore is Associate Professor of Theatre at Queens College of the City University of New York. He edited, with Ruby Cohn, TWENTIETH CENTURY DRAMA: ENGLAND, IRELAND, UNITED STATES (Random House, 1966) and is currently at work on BERNARD SHAW'S SCREENPLAY OF *SAINT JOAN* for the University of Washington Press and INTRODUCTION TO LITERATURE, with Samuel Woods and Mary Rohrberger, for Random House. He has published articles on Bernard Shaw, Tennessee Williams, and various aspects of modern drama and European theater in TULANE DRAMA REVIEW, MODERN DRAMA, EDUCATION THEATRE JOURNAL, and other periodicals. He is presently Associate Editor of EDUCATIONAL THEATRE JOURNAL.

Weller Embler is Professor of English at The Cooper Union for the Advancement of Science and Art, in New York City. A scholar in the field of contemporary literature, he has contributed numerous articles to journals and anthologies. His book, METAPHOR AND MEANING (Everett/Edwards, inc., 1966) explores the use of metaphor in contemporary literature, art, and social philosophy and has been widely acclaimed by reviewers as an original contribution to semantics and criticism.

Donna Gerstenberger is Associate Professor of English at the University of Washington, Seattle, Washington. She is the author of JOHN MILLINGTON SYNGE (1964) and, with George Hend-

187

rick, of SECOND DIRECTORY OF PERIODICALS PUBLISHING ARTICLES IN ENGLISH AND AMERICAN LANGUAGE AND LITERATURE (1965) and THE AMERICAN NOVEL 1789-1959: A CHECKLIST OF TWENTIETH CENTURY CRITICISM (2nd. ed. rev., 1962), and has contributed widely to periodicals, including MODERN DRAMA, CRITICISM, COLLEGE ENGLISH, WESTERN HUMANITIES REVIEW, MODERN FICTION STUDIES, and MODERN LANGUAGE NOTES. She has been editor of ABSTRACTS OF ENGLISH STUDIES since 1958.

Jay L. Halio is Professor of English at the University of California at Davis. He is the author of a book on the British writer Angus Wilson. He also writes on Shakespeare and the Elizabethans and is currently working on critical, old-spelling editions of MACBETH and KING LEAR. Some of his criticism has appeared in SOUTHERN REVIEW, MODERN FICTION STUDIES, COLLEGE ENGLISH, SHAKESPEARE QUARTERLY, NEOPHILOLOGUS, and ENGLISH LANGUAGE NOTES.

Max Halperen is Professor of English at North Carolina State University. He has published articles on Dylan Thomas and Ezra Pound. He is an associate editor of SOUTHERN POETRY REVIEW.

Sy Kahn is Professor of English at Raymond College, University of the Pacific. A prolific poet and scholar-critic, he has published four volumes of poetry, essays on Glenway Wescott, F. Scott Fitzgerald, Harry Crosby, Kenneth Fearing, and Stephen Crane. He is presently at work on three books, one on Harry Crosby, one on Kenneth Fearing, and one on Maxwell Bodenheim. He is active as a reader of poetry in public performance and has his own poetry-jazz group, which is much in demand on college campuses and community theaters.

Louis Phillips teaches English at the Maritime College of the City of New York. He is a widely published poet, is poetry editor of GRAFFITI, a magazine of the arts, and is active in experimental theater and film projects in New York City.

R. Baird Shuman is professor of Education at Duke University. He is a poet, and has published over one hundred scholarly articles in such journals as PMLA, THE ENGLISH JOURNAL, SOUTH ATLANTIC QUARTERLY and MODERN PHILOLOGY. He is the author of three volumes of dramatic criticism, all published by Twayne Publishers: CLIFFORD ODETS (1962; reprinted, 1964); ROBERT E. SHERWOOD (1964; reprinted, 1965); and WILLIAM INGE (1965; reprinted, 1966).

Alan A. Stambusky is Associate Professor of Dramatic Art at the University of California, Davis. His publications include articles in DRAMA CRITIQUE, DRAMATISTS GUILD QUARTERLY, LOCK HAVEN REVIEW, EDUCATIONAL THEATER JOURNAL, QUARTERLY JOURNAL OF SPEECH, and THE SPEECH TEACHER. He is presently at work on a book on the origins and development of censorship of the drama.

William E. Taylor is Professor of English at Stetson University. He has published two volumes of poems, was co-editor, with Richare E. Langford, of THE TWENTIES: POETRY AND PROSE (Everett/Edwards, inc., 1966), and has had a one-act play published in POET LORE and a full length drama performed at Stover Theater, Stetson University. He was editor for four years of the poetry page of the Florida Education Association Journal and has started publishing his own poetry magazine POETRY FLORIDA AND. He has written articles on Tennessee Williams, Eugene O'-Neill, and Clifford Odets. He is on the Board of Reviewers for THE WORLD IN BOOKS.

Index